"Bil Cornelius is a man of zeal and passion for [...] in his life and the lives of the people around him. As a pastor, mentor, and leader he has devoted his life to helping others realize that today is the day for embracing your purpose in Christ."

—**Steven Furtick**, lead pastor, Elevation Church; author of the *New York Times* bestseller *Greater*

"If you have a dream and don't know where to start, you have the right book in your hands. Bil Cornelius will walk you through the process of hearing from God and taking the right steps to achieve your dreams and more. What are you waiting for? Today is the day!"

—**Craig Groeschel**, senior pastor, LifeChurch.tv; author of *Altar Ego* and *Becoming Who God Says You Are*

"Life and reality have a tendency to push the dreams God gives us aside in favor of conventional, logical living. *Today Is the Day* not only gives you the tools to dream big but also challenges you to put principles into action, see your dreams become reality, and believe that God can do bigger miracles than you could ever imagine."

—**Robert Morris,** founding senior pastor, Gateway Church; bestselling author of *The Blessed Life*, *From Dream to Destiny*, and *The God I Never Knew*

"What do you need to make your dream a reality? What excuses have held you back? We are all capable of having the life God designed for us, and in *Today Is the Day* Bil Cornelius inspires us to go for it! If you want to reignite the dreams in your heart or identify new ones, read on!"

—**Perry Noble**, senior pastor, Newspring Church

"Bil sent me *Today Is the Day* at a time when I was beginning a new business endeavor in my life. He lays out a faith-based plan to approach a goal or dream while inspiring you to take the steps to make your dream become reality. Ready to jump? Today is the day!"

—**Rich Franklin**, three-time UFC champion

"Bil Cornelius is relentless in pursuing God-sized dreams and turning them into reality. If you have a dream, think bigger. If you've been wishing the dream would come to pass, start taking action now. Bil has lived this out and has written a book that will equip you to do the same. *Today Is the Day* is like a turbo charge to your dreams!"

—**Stovall Weems**, lead pastor, Celebration Church

"Every dream starts somewhere. It begins as a thought that grows into a passion. But how can you make the most of that dream? How can you see that passion become reality? In his newest book, my good friend Bil Cornelius uncovers a reality that your dream— no matter what it is—can become reality. Anyone who ever had a 'someday' dream needs to read this book. Because realizing your dream isn't about thinking of what might be someday. It's all about understanding and following God's plan for your life now and making the most of the day God has given you—today!"

—**Ed Young**, pastor, Fellowship Church; author, *Outrageous, Contagious Joy*

TODAY
IS
THE DAY

TODAY
IS
THE DAY

FIND AND EMBRACE YOUR GOD-GIVEN DREAMS

BIL CORNELIUS

with James Pence

BakerBooks

a division of Baker Publishing Group
Grand Rapids, Michigan

© 2014 by Bil Cornelius

Published by Baker Books
a division of Baker Publishing Group
P.O. Box 6287, Grand Rapids, MI 49516-6287
www.bakerbooks.com

Paperback edition published 2014
ISBN 978-0-8010-1668-4

Printed in the United States of America

The Library of Congress has cataloged the original edition as follows:
Cornelius, Bil, 1972–
    Today is the day : find and embrace your God-given purpose / Bil Cornelius, with James Pence.
        page cm
    Includes bibliographical references and index.
    ISBN 978-0-8010-1524-3 (cloth : alk. paper)
    1. Dreams—Religious aspects—Christianity. 2. Change (Psychology)—Religious aspects—Christianity. 3. Success—Religious aspects—Christianity. 4. Self-actualization (Psychology)—Religious aspects—Christianity. I. Title.
    BR115.D74C68 2014
    248.4—dc23   2013029556

14   15   16   17   18   19   20   7   6   5   4   3   2   1

Contents

Contents

Part 3 Moving to the Next Level

Acknowledgments

Writing a book is a giant undertaking that involves a team of people. I am forever indebted to the following people who helped make this project a reality.

Thank you to Tom Winters and Debby Boyd, for believing in the project and seeing it through to the end.

To Baker Books, especially Chad Allen and Kristin Kornoelje, for your patience with me in putting my thoughts in the right order.

To Jim Pence, for helping take my thoughts and make sense of them for the reader.

To Bay Area Fellowship, the first to hear this content . . . and the best church in the world! (I'm a little biased.)

To my volunteer team of editors at Bay Area Fellowship: Paul Schulz, Dee Dee Sharon, Bryan Fiscus, and Alisa Wagner.

To the marketing teams at Bay Area Fellowship and Baker Books, who help get the word out on a book like this so that all our efforts do not get lost in a sea of books sitting on bookstore shelves and never reach the reader.

To my amazing family: Mason and Cole, my two boys who are growing into men right in front of me, and my beautiful daughter

Sophie, who knows she has her daddy wrapped around her finger. And to my best friend and amazing wife, Jessica, who has proven to be the best deal I've ever made. Convincing her to marry me is a daily example of God's awesome power and grace upon my life.

And thank you, God, for sending your Son to save me and to give me a purpose beyond words, and for filling my life with such promise and opportunity!

Introduction

I'd like to ask you two questions. First, if you could do anything, what would it be? In other words, what is your purpose in life, your dream? Second, what are you doing to fulfill that purpose?

Unfortunately, many of us never do anything to see our dreams, the purposes in our hearts, realized. We coast through life, wishing things were different but never doing anything to change. Sometimes we toss out excuses. "I don't have enough money." "There's not enough time." "I've tried and failed so many times that I've just given up." Eventually, we give in to discouragement and convince ourselves that nothing in our lives will ever change.

Sound familiar?

If it does, I'd like to come alongside and help. In fact, nothing would give me more joy or pleasure than for you to find a fulfilling and fruitful life. In this book, I am going to share with you some steps that work without fail.

Why should you listen to me? I've been there. I grew up in a normal Christian home with great parents. Later, I attended college and seminary and went into the ministry. But there was a problem. I loved God and lived for him, but I felt surprisingly unfulfilled. How was that possible? I had bought into a lie that well-meaning Christians had told me, but it was something Jesus never said. Here's the lie: if you love God and are devoted to him, you'll automatically be happy and fulfilled.

Not true.

It is possible to love God and still miss all he has for you. In my own experience, God showed me the difference between a power-less Christian life (where people talk big about everything God "can do" but rarely see much of it) and a life of actually seeing God do amazing things in and through his people.

With God's help, I was able to take hold of my circumstances and create the life I always wanted, and I'm no more gifted or smarter than you. Both human history and Scripture show that you are capable of having a life that consists of much more than you can currently dream or imagine.

Through the principles I describe in this book, I have:

- created a marriage and family filled with joy
- started a church for the unchurched in South Texas that has grown to over nine thousand people and ten campuses
- acquired over one million dollars in real estate, creating cash flow that rivals a full-time income
- become a bestselling author despite the fact that I was in remedial reading classes up to tenth grade and had to go to an open enrollment college because I tested so poorly
- become a paid consultant to executives, nonprofit orga-nizations, and pastors, being paid three to five thousand dol-lars over a one- or two-day period to share the same concepts I'm explaining in this book

These principles are not only for businesspeople. What I share in this book is the same thing I tell everybody, whether I'm talking with a businessman who owns a headhunting firm, a single mother who's trying to figure out how to put her life back together after a devastating divorce, or a nineteen-year-old college student who says, "I want my life to count. What should I do?"

I hope you'll keep reading, because God wants to do great things in your life too. You may not share my particular dreams, and that's okay. God gave you dreams of your own to accomplish.

It's time to take hold of your future. You can't change your past, but if you listen and apply the biblical principles in this book, I promise a better future awaits you.

Today is the day to get started on those dreams.

Part 1

DISCOVERING
Your God-Given Dreams

1

Is My Dream
FROM GOD?

· · · · ·

We all have dreams. Some of them are merely whims, while others are burning needs we must fulfill. I'm guessing you picked up this book because you want more out of life. Maybe you feel frustrated that life is passing you by. Or perhaps well-meaning people are throwing cold water on your dreams, telling you to "be realistic." Whatever your desires, I believe they are there for a reason. More than that, I believe if you have dreams, God has pre-wired you for them.

What do I mean by that?

As a gift, a friend of mine who works in construction built a house for my family at a discount. When he designed it for us, he included certain amenities that we didn't even consider. As the builder and creator of the home, he knew we would want these things after the fact, so he put them in for us. For example, he pre-wired our home for cable and internet. We didn't request this, but he knew we would want it once we moved in. Similarly, God has pre-wired us with what he knows we need to live full lives.

When I was a kid, my parents took me to church all the time. I thought it was normal to go to church on Sunday morning, afternoon, and night! On top of that, I went to Wednesday night youth group, as well as small group meetings on Monday or Tuesday night. Because our church didn't have its own building yet, my dad and I volunteered on Friday nights to set up the church in an elementary school. At the time, I had no idea God was preparing me to start my own church one day and to spend my life training other people to start churches.

Do you see how God worked? He gave me a background and a family that were part of a church plant. Then he pre-wired me with a desire to help others start churches. God gave me the desire of my heart.

The book of Psalms tells us, "Take delight in the LORD, and he will give you the desires of your heart" (Ps. 37:4). *Your* heart. Not your mother's or your father's heart. Not your high school guidance counselor's heart. Your heart.

What has God put on your heart? If you were free to dream and to do whatever your heart desires, what would you do? Or to put it as author Brian Dozeman does, "What would you do if you knew you couldn't fail?"[1] How you answer this question is a good indication of how you have been pre-wired.

Right about now you may be asking, "How do I know whether my desire is just a selfish whim or if it's really something God wants me to pursue?" The story of a guy in the Bible named Nehemiah is a great example of how to determine whether your dream is from God.

Nehemiah was working for a king in Persia when friends and family from Jerusalem visited and told him that his hometown was in trouble. Nehemiah wrote, "Hanani, one of my brothers, came to visit me with some other men who had just arrived from Judah. . . . They said to me, 'Things are not going well for those who returned to the province of Judah. . . . The wall of Jerusalem has been torn down, and the gates have been destroyed by fire.' When I heard this, I sat down and wept. In fact, for days I mourned, fasted, and prayed to the God of heaven" (Neh. 1:2–4 NLT).

In those days, a city's wall was its protection. If the wall was broken down, the people were vulnerable to attack. Today it would be like living in a high-crime area with no doors on your house. Even though Nehemiah lived far away from Jerusalem and was safe and secure, he felt deeply burdened for his people. The desire of his heart was to rebuild the wall.

As you look at how he responded to the bad news from home, you'll see eight clues for how to test and validate the desires of your heart.

Clue 1

A God-Given Dream Will Be Powerful and Persistent

A God-given dream is "sticky." A dream that is only a neat idea will fade.

Have you ever gotten something sticky, like gum, on your hands? The more you try to get it off, the more it spreads. That's the way a desire from God works. First, you have an idea; then the idea has you. You can't stop thinking about it. You search for it on Google. You read books about it. You talk about it. You may even order some teaching videos or attend a seminar on it. And, like Nehemiah, you may feel so compelled that you begin to pray about it.

When Nehemiah learned that the wall of Jerusalem was broken down, he prayed—and kept praying. "Let your ear be attentive and your eyes open to hear the prayer your servant is praying before you day and night" (Neh. 1:6).

What makes you come alive on the inside? What is that thing you do that gets you fired up at the mere thought of spending time doing it? For me, it was teaching others and leading as a pastor. That's what I wanted to do more than anything in the world. For you, it may be working with your hands, building things for people. Or maybe you have a heart for the homeless. Maybe music is your passion, and you love to sing or play for people. Everyone has something they are naturally or, as I believe, *supernaturally* drawn to.

What is God drawing you to do?

Clue 2

A God-Given Dream Will Solve Problems for Others

God has wired us to solve a problem for someone else. Nehemiah knew Jerusalem was exposed to the danger of enemy attackers because the city wall was broken down. He wanted to solve that problem so badly that it became a consuming passion.

As I've already mentioned, one of my dreams is to help people plant churches. Believe me, when you start a new church, you're going to have a lot of challenges. It goes with the territory. Because I've faced those problems myself, I want to help others solve them. You may not be the least bit interested in church planting, but you like to work with your hands. If you do, people like me need you. I can't fix anything!

God designed us to serve others. Peter (one of Jesus's disciples) wrote, "God has given each of you a gift from his great variety of spiritual gifts. Use them well to serve one another" (1 Pet. 4:10 NLT). God made us to be difference makers.

Do you know someone with a problem that needs solving? God wants to use you to make a difference.

A God-Given Dream Will Include a Burden for People

When you're thinking about your dream, the question isn't always, "What do you want to do or become?" Often the question is, "If you could do this or become that, *who could you help in the process*?" As a pastor, I want to help people. A pastor helps people, but so does a mechanic, a mom, a teacher, a volunteer at a local mission, or an entrepreneur who provides a product or service that meets the needs of his customers and provides jobs for others.

Nehemiah, like all those whom God uses greatly, met the needs of God's people, but before he could do this, he had to have a burden for them. Nehemiah wanted to help the people living in Jerusalem to be safe. He also wanted to remove the humiliation and disgrace the Israelites lived with because

> **Everyone has something they are naturally or, as I believe, *supernaturally* drawn to.**

the wall of their capital city was broken down. That desire became the driving force behind everything else Nehemiah did. It moved him to pray, to go out on a limb and make outrageous requests of his boss, to risk his life in a dangerous journey, and to take on a seemingly impossible task.

Whom are you burdened for? Whom would you like to reach out to and help? The answer will help you identify your God-given dream.

Clue 4

A God-Given Dream Will Involve Access

What do I mean by *access*?

Have you ever noticed how many NFL quarterbacks have fathers who were coaches? Access. How many actors do you know of who have family in the business? Access.

Nehemiah had access. He had personal connections to Jerusalem, and he wanted the wall to be rebuilt to protect his family.

> **If God can design the world and make you and me, don't you think he is smart enough to put us in close proximity to the things we need to learn to make our dreams a reality?**

But Nehemiah also worked for a king as his cupbearer. A cupbearer tasted the king's food and wine before the king ate or drank to make sure no one was trying to poison the king (kings were pretty paranoid people). This gave Nehemiah direct access to executive leadership. He had the opportunity to observe how the king managed people, handled large projects, and deployed resources.

Even more important, because he was a trusted member of the king's court (you've got to have a lot of faith in the person who's keeping you from being poisoned), Nehemiah was able to ask the king for some perks. He requested an armed guard to protect him as he traveled, and he even asked the king to supply materials for the construction project (Neh. 2:7–8). God gave Nehemiah not only a purpose but also access to the experience, training, and resources he would need to fulfill that purpose.

How about you? Has God been preparing you in advance for a particular task? Maybe you stumbled upon your dream when you saw something on a class trip. Or perhaps something within you came alive when you were watching a movie or reading an article. Maybe you already have direct or indirect connections to the inside workings of a business or trade. God has given you access to these experiences and connections for a reason: to fulfill his dream for you.

If God can design the world and make you and me, don't you think he is smart enough to put us in close proximity to the things we need to learn to make our dreams a reality? This doesn't mean you already know everything you need to know, but it does mean you know enough to declare your dream and get started.

Clue 5

A God-Given Dream Will Help God's Work in the World

Nehemiah dreamed of rebuilding the wall around Jerusalem. This wall not only would protect his family and God's people but also would help in the rebuilding of the temple. In those days, the wall of a city was also used as a cornerstone for other buildings, whether it be a temple or someone's house. By repairing Jerusalem's wall, Nehemiah played a key part in rebuilding the temple and restoring the worship of God to the nation. Others would complete that work, but his part was crucial.

Maybe you have a hard time seeing how your dream goes beyond improving your own life. Ask yourself this: "If I succeed at this, will I have more influence or affluence to be able to do more for God?" Consider the possibility that your dream is part of the kingdom of God. As long as your dream does not go against God's Word, you may be onto God's will for your life. This is one of the reasons the Bible says, "The kingdom of God is within you."

Clue 6

A God-Given Dream Will Grow from Your Abilities and Talents

God gave you abilities and talents. He will not ask you to do something he has not equipped you to do. For example, if you do not have the ability to get up in front of others and speak, you are probably not called to be a senior pastor. If you are not good with people, it's doubtful God would call you to manage people. If you're not athletic, you probably should give up the dream of being a star quarterback in the NFL.

This clue may seem obvious, but it isn't always. Some people's dreams are actually an attempt to make up for one of their weaknesses. Don't try to make up for your weaknesses; instead, focus on your strengths. Then you can let God fill in your weak spots through others who are strong in those areas.

Nehemiah had a dream to rebuild the wall of Jerusalem. But if you read his story, you'll notice that he didn't try to do all the building himself (see Neh. 2:16–17). Nehemiah was a leader, a planner, an organizer, a visionary. He allowed God to use his strengths to help accomplish his dream, but he also relied on other people for the actual construction work.

We all need one another. Focus on your core competencies, the talents and abilities God has given you, and you're on your way to discovering your God-given dream.

Clue 7

A God-Given Dream May Grow Out of Adversity

Have you ever heard the adage "Your misery can become your ministry"? Nehemiah could relate to misery. The thought of his people being vulnerable, living in Jerusalem without protection, plagued him. He was frustrated, unable to shake the need to do something. And with that frustration, a dream was forming.

Nehemiah wrote down his reaction to the bad news from home. "They said to me, 'Things are not going well. . . . The wall of Jerusalem has been torn down.' . . . When I heard this, I sat down and wept. In fact, for days I mourned, fasted, and prayed to the God of heaven" (Neh. 1:3–4 NLT).

> If you feel frustrated with your current situation, perhaps that frustration is there not to paralyze you but to drive you to action.

Nehemiah did not sit around and worry about the situation. And he didn't just send up a quick prayer, "Lord, help those people," and then forget about it. He decided to take on the task of rebuilding the wall. He took his misery and made it his mission.

The story of King David provides another illustration of how God can use difficult circumstances to cultivate a dream. David knew he was destined to become the next king (1 Sam. 16:1), but he probably had no idea how difficult the road to the throne of Israel would be. One of the ways God developed David into a great king was by putting him under a lousy king named Saul. After David killed Goliath, Saul felt so threatened that he practically went crazy. One minute Saul was leaning on David for help, the next he was throwing spears at him. David had to flee for his life and live in the desert, but during that time, God built into him the qualities of a king.

If you feel frustrated with your current situation, perhaps that frustration is there not to paralyze you but to drive you to action. I know several people who made it their goal to be extremely wealthy because they grew up in poverty. Several men in my church dream of being amazing dads because they had bad fathers. One of my dreams is to support church planters and train them because, back when our church was getting started, we were so broke and I had very few pastors to talk to for advice. I want to be the resource I never had.

What are you struggling with? What difficulties weigh you down right now? Consider them carefully, because they may be the seeds of your God-given dream.

Clue 8

A God-Given Dream May Seem (to Others) Crazy or Arrogant

Often we fail to pursue our dreams because we're afraid people will think we're proud or arrogant. Our parents or pastors taught us to be humble, and it goes against the grain to put ourselves forward or pursue a dream. Rather than stepping out and doing something great, in the name of humility, we step back and do nothing.

I am a firm believer in humility; however, we often confuse humility with passivity. Humility isn't about sitting back and doing nothing. Humility is about recognizing our limits and knowing that everything we have comes from God. Arrogance or pride, on the other hand, is an attitude of superiority. It's the attitude that says, "I don't need God. I can do this myself."

I want to suggest something that may go against what well-meaning friends or family members may have taught you. If your dream seems crazy or daring, this may be an indication it's a God-given dream. We serve a big God. You cannot achieve great things by thinking small.

If God gave you your dream, chances are it's so big that you are probably embarrassed to tell people out of fear they will think you are prideful. If that's true of you, consider the words of Rick Warren, pastor of one of the largest churches in the United States: "Never make your plans based on how big you think you are, but on how big you think God is."[2] Nehemiah thought big. He wanted to take on one of the largest construction projects Jerusalem had ever seen. He knew it was a God-sized project.

When my wife and I first moved to Corpus Christi, I came with a big dream. I went around our city asking anyone and everyone to join us for a core group meeting (a small Bible study that would eventually turn into a church). Two weeks after we moved into a small, two-bedroom apartment, we had our first meeting.

Five people attended.

At that meeting, I announced, "This is not a Bible study. This is the beginning of a church that will one day reach thousands of people!"

After the meeting, my wife said, "Bil, please don't say that. These people are going to think you're crazy!"

It's not that my wife didn't believe in the dream. In fact, she was and is my biggest supporter. She was trying to protect me. She didn't want others to think badly of me or to write me off as some kind of kook. Nevertheless, I don't regret making such a bold claim, because what I said was true. Jesus told his followers, "What you say flows from what is in your heart" (Luke 6:45 NLT). God knew my heart.

In the fourteen years since I spoke those words, we have seen that vision unfold. God allowed the dream he gave me to become a reality. Now that our church has ten campuses and over nine thousand people attending, my bold statement has become a part of our history.

Some people probably thought Nehemiah was crazy when he left an important job with the king of Persia and traveled nearly a thousand miles over dangerous terrain to rebuild the wall of a city that had lain in ruins for over seventy years. But Nehemiah didn't care. He had a daring, outrageous, God-given dream, and because of that dream, he undertook a mammoth task.

Do you know what happened?

Not only did Nehemiah and his compatriots rebuild the wall of Jerusalem, but they did it in record time. Without any modern equipment or technology, they completed the task in fifty-two days. On top of that, Nehemiah ultimately became the governor of Jerusalem (see Neh. 6:15; 10:1). How's that for seeing a crazy dream fulfilled?

Has someone told you that you can't follow the desire of your heart? Have you been saying that to yourself? It's time to quit listening to the nay-saying voices, external or internal, that are keeping you from your God-given dream. It's time to declare your dream and get started on making it become a reality.

• • •

This book won't be much help to you unless you put into practice the principles I am sharing. At the end of each chapter, I'm going to give you a practical action step. You may want to use a notebook or journal as you work through these steps so you'll be able to keep your thoughts organized and refer back to them.

Find a quiet place where you won't be disturbed and write down your dreams. Write them all down and don't worry (for the time being) about explaining why you have them or where they came from. The important thing right now is to get them down on paper. Ready? Go.

1.

2.

3.

4.

5.

2

Think Big, Then
THINK BIGGER

• • • • •

In his audio training series *The Ten-Minute Coach*, Dan Lier tells about when, as a young salesman, he went to interview a top seller in his field. The man was about the same age as Dan, yet he was earning over $250,000 a year—more than twice what Dan was making. After talking with Dan for a few minutes, the successful salesman said something that startled him.

He said, "Dan, please don't take this wrong, but you will never sell enough of your product to earn $250,000 a year."

Trying not to be offended, Dan asked him what he meant.

The young salesman replied, "It's not that I'm trying to limit you, but you will never make $250,000 a year with that $100,000 a year attitude you walked in here with."

Dan was shocked, but he learned a valuable lesson that day. The starting point to the next level of income, or anything else for that matter, is not in skill or knowledge but in learning to think big.[1]

Most of us sell ourselves short by thinking too small. Whether because of a fear of failure or a desire to appear humble, we try to get by with scaled-down dreams that appear achievable. But have you ever taken the time to think about what it means to have a God-given dream?

Listen to what the Old Testament prophet Amos says about God: "He who forms the mountains, who creates the wind, and who reveals his thoughts to mankind, who turns dawn to darkness, and treads on the heights of the earth—the LORD God Almighty is his name" (Amos 4:13). Isn't that awesome? The God who created the heavens, the earth, and the seas also gave you your dreams. The same God who set the mountains in place placed desires in your heart. The size of your dream matters to him.

> **The same God who set the mountains in place placed desires in your heart.**

Unfortunately, most of us tend to downsize our dreams so that we have a better chance of achieving them. The problem is that when we shrink our dreams down to something doable, we weaken them. The dreams may feel less intimidating, but they also will be less inspiring. In fact, they may not be inspiring at all. God wants our dreams to fill us with enthusiasm, to motivate us to get out of bed in the morning. God wants to give us a dream greater than ourselves.

What does that kind of dream look like? Here's a hint. It'll be so big that when you talk about it, you'll want to laugh out loud.

Laugh-Out-Loud Bigness

You can find people with these God-given, laugh-out-loud dreams throughout the Bible, but one of my favorites is a man named Abraham. God spoke to him in his old age and told him he would become the father of a great nation. That posed a major problem for Abraham because he was childless. On top of that, he was pushing a hundred years old. To make matters worse, his wife was ninety and had never been able to have children.

Now, try putting yourself in Abraham's place. God appears to you and tells you that, at almost one hundred years old, you're going to have a child by your ninety-year-old wife. Not only that, but this child will have enough descendants to become an entire nation. How do you think you'd react?

The book of Genesis tells us that Abraham laughed. "But he [Abraham] laughed to himself in disbelief. 'How could I become a father at the age of 100?' he thought. 'And how can Sarah have a baby when she is ninety years old?'" (Gen. 17:17 NLT).

Abraham wasn't the only one who laughed. His wife, Sarah, did too. One chapter later, we read, "So she [Sarah] laughed silently to herself and said, 'How could a worn-out woman like me enjoy such pleasure, especially when my master—my husband—is also so old?'" (Gen. 18:12 NLT).

This dream that God gave Abraham was so crazy, so outlandish, that if it came true, God would receive all the glory. There was no way Abraham and Sarah could fulfill this dream themselves, and that was the whole point. Right after Sarah laughed at God's promise, God asked Abraham, "Why did Sarah laugh? . . . Is anything too hard for the LORD?" (Gen. 18:13–14 NLT).

> **God wants to take you from laughing at your dream to actually believing it's possible.**

God wants to take you from laughing at your dream to actually believing it's possible. Consider how big your dream really is and hear the words God spoke to Abraham. "Is anything too hard for the LORD?"

Get Close to Something Big

God also communicated the bigness of his promise to Abraham by giving him a visual illustration—something big to compare it to. One night, God told Abraham to go outside and to look up into the sky. Then he told him to try to count the stars. There was no such thing as light pollution back then, so Abraham could see a lot more stars than we can. When Abraham looked up into the sky, it was filled with thousands and thousands of stars.

Abraham couldn't have counted them. There were too many. As Abraham gazed up into the star-filled sky, God dropped a bomb on him: "That's how many descendants you will have!" (Gen. 15:5 NLT). For a childless man in the twilight of his life, that was a huge dream.

God wants to give you a huge dream too. God will give you a vision, a mental picture of something big in which he wants you to play the lead role. He will give you a film, a movie in your mind's eye, of the part you are to play in his kingdom, a part that will bring him glory when the end credits of your life roll.

How do you get that mental picture? Abraham stepped outside to get a view of his God-given dream of fathering a nation, and a change of location can help you too.

I want to encourage you to get in your car and drive to something big. Maybe you live close to the ocean. Maybe you are within minutes of a mountaintop in the Colorado Rockies. Maybe you can gain access to a large stadium and ask if you can just sit in the stands while you take a few moments to read the rest of this chapter. Or try Googling "ocean" or "stadium" or "mountaintop" or "night sky" and view an inspiring image on your computer.

A friend of mine named Joel Malm teaches leaders to think bigger by taking them on large-scale mountain hikes. He once told me what author and speaker Mark Batterson told him about these events: "Change of place plus change of pace equals change of perspective."

A few years ago, I went to a friend's church in Houston, Texas. I entered the empty auditorium on a weekday, found a seat, and with sixteen thousand seats in front of me, I took the time to dream some big dreams. Another time, when I was speaking at a conference in New Jersey, I asked my host if he would take me to Atlantic City. He readily agreed, and we had dinner near the boardwalk. Then I asked if he would give me a tour of one of Donald Trump's landmark properties, the Trump Taj Mahal. Even though I don't gamble, I wanted to walk through the facility, just to be inspired by someone's big dream. Take some time to find a structure—manmade or God-made—that is huge, and as you scope out the vast size of it, ask God out loud, "God, am I dreaming big enough?"

Five Questions to Help You Think Bigger

Since most of us are conditioned to scale down our dreams, we often face a steep learning curve when we're trying to think big. Sometimes it helps to ask ourselves some leading questions as we cultivate big dreams.

Our brains are truly amazing. Whatever questions we ask, our minds will answer. But we have to make sure we're asking the right questions if we want to get the right answers. For example, if you ask yourself, "Why am I such a loser?" your mind will find reasons. But if you turn that question on its head and ask, "Why am I such a winner?" you may be surprised at the good answers you come up with.

Let's get our amazing minds working for us and not against us. Here are five questions that will help.

1. If you had all the money in the world, what would you do?

Often we allow money to stop us before we even start. We sense God speaking to us, leading us into something big. Then we say to ourselves, "I can't afford that!" With that simple response, our big idea evaporates.

Remember that God provides everything you need for the journey, so never start with the money question. The apostle Paul once reminded some Christians, "This same God who takes care of me will supply all your needs from his glorious riches, which have been given to us in Christ Jesus" (Phil. 4:19 NLT). Start by assuming that all the resources you need for the dream will come as you need them. Simply dream big as if God were rich—because he is.

2. If you had all the time in the world, what would you do?

Sometimes we set aside our dreams because we feel we don't have the time to work on them. Maybe you feel like you are starting too late in life for a big dream to happen for you. (If that's the case, you may want to check out Abraham's and Sarah's ages again.) Maybe your children's busy schedules keep you running from soccer to ballet to piano and so on. Perhaps your work schedule is so full that you barely have enough time to sleep, let alone cultivate a dream.

If any of the above scenarios sound familiar, ask yourself this: "If time were no longer a factor—if I had all the time in the world—what would I do?" As you think about what you'd do with that much time, remember that you always have enough time to do God's will. If he's giving you a dream, he will give you the time you need to accomplish it.

3. If you could talk to the most successful person in your field of interest (dead or alive), what do you suppose his or her advice to you would be?

This is one of my favorite questions to ask. It's a practical question too, because often you can read books by people you admire and discover exactly what they would tell you to do. When I'm dreaming about my ministry, I often ask, "What would Ed Young, Craig Groeschel, Bishop T. D. Jakes, Joel Osteen, or Rick Warren tell me?" These pastors think big, and I want to learn from them.

When I am considering a business or real estate deal, I'll ask myself, "What would Donald Trump or Jack Welch suggest?" Thinking about these men and what they've accomplished always makes me think bigger. When I'm in prayer and seeking God, I ask, "What would Bruce Wilkinson, Andrew Murray, or Charles Spurgeon say about the spiritual need I'm facing?"

Whom do you admire? Whose success would you like to emulate? Read some of their books. Visit their websites. Study their lives and accomplishments. Then hold a mock dialogue with them in your mind. Sit down and pick their brains for ideas and suggestions on how to dream big.

4. If you knew you couldn't fail, what would you attempt for God?

Fear of failure is a major reason why people scale down their dreams or choose not to try. But if we set aside our dreams without trying, we've guaranteed failure.

What if failure was not even a possibility? What if you had an imaginary safety net under you that guaranteed success? What would you try to do for God? What business or ministry would you start? If you couldn't be rejected, what new position or job would you apply for?

Right now I'm not asking you to go out and *do* anything. I just want you to learn how to think big—then think bigger.

5. What do you secretly want that you are too embarrassed to tell anyone about?

Another reason we scale down or fail to attempt our dreams is that we're worried about what people will think or say. We don't want to be vulnerable. We don't want to risk the possibility that our friends or loved ones will laugh at us. And so, deep down, we harbor secret desires, secret dreams that we keep between ourselves and God.

The Bible speaks of the secret petitions of the heart and says that God knows those secrets. Not only is he aware of them, but he also promises to grant those desires to us if we love him. The book of Psalms tells us, "Take delight in the LORD, and he will give you the desires of your heart" (Ps. 37:4).

As you grow closer to God and surrender yourself fully to his will, which of your desires do you find increasing? What desires are not going away? What are the dreams you are dying to act on? Which dreams fall in line with your gifts, and what do you believe God is leading you to do? If you knew people wouldn't laugh at you, what dream would you share with them?

Add a Zero

In this chapter, we've been learning to think big, but for a moment I want you to do just the opposite. Shrink your dream to a number or size that causes you to lose interest in it.

For example, I dream of pastoring a dynamic, growing, world-impacting church with more than ten thousand people in attendance every weekend. If I shrink that congregation down to a few hundred, the dream loses its appeal. I'm not excited about it anymore. But what if I were to take that same church and add a zero, making it one hundred thousand people? Now I'm excited! Reducing the size of my dream causes me to lose interest, while multiplying it tenfold makes me want to get up and shout.

Think about what happened in the book of Acts on the day of Pentecost. Peter preached one sermon, and three thousand people were saved (Acts 2:41). Notice it wasn't three, or thirty, or even three hundred. It was three thousand. That's a size that is impossible to explain apart from God.

So what's your supernatural number? Do you want to own a restaurant? How about ten franchises of that same restaurant? Or one hundred?

At times, even spirituality can be quantified. Whenever I sensed God challenging me to grow in Christ, I felt led to quantify my prayer time. You may be thinking, "Prayer is not about the numbers. It's about quality, not quantity." In the past, I would have agreed with you. But it wasn't until after I committed to praying a massive amount of time (more about this later) that I experienced the wonder of God's presence in a powerful way. Had I continued giving him a small quantity of time, I'm not sure that would have happened.

If you want to make your dream exciting, consider adding a zero to it. See if this does not make you smile with possibilities. What if instead of setting a goal of earning one hundred thousand dollars this year from your sales job, you make it your goal to be able to give that amount to God's work at the end of the year? It's amazing what a well-placed zero can do.

My good friend Joe McArthur decided one day to add a zero to his dreams. Joe leads our student ministry, and a few years back, attendance averaged around three hundred students at our broadcast campus on any given weekend. Then something happened that challenged him to dream bigger. Joe was introduced to the student ministry pastors of Hillsong Church, and they invited him to attend Two52, an event for students that they were speaking at.

As Joe explains it, on the last night of the event, God was clearly moving. Several thousand students attended the service, and at the end, the speaker invited them to come forward and to make a decision to follow Christ or to recommit their lives to Christ. As the band played, hundreds upon hundreds of students came forward, giving themselves fully to Christ.

As this was happening, one of the leaders of the event told Joe to go on stage. Joe was hesitant because he wasn't on the program. Nevertheless, he walked onto the stage and asked the speaker leading the event, "What do you want me to say or do?"

The speaker replied, "Nothing. Just stand here and watch all the students giving themselves to God. Then allow God to get big in your heart."

As Joe watched student after student come forward, crying, worshiping, and praying, something changed in him. He came back to our church with bigness in his heart. Within a few weeks, God led Joe to announce that he had a vision of something big like Two52 happening in our youth group. When he shared his dream with me, with his youth team, and with the students, it took on a life of its own. The next thing I knew, a date was set for an event called Awaken. But instead of hosting the event in the youth room (which seats three hundred), Joe decided to hold the event on two weeknights in the main auditorium (which seats twenty-seven hundred).

He added a zero.

The students got excited and began to Facebook, tweet, and call their friends. The church prayed, and the student team prepared. With no formal advertising and no big-name bands or speakers, the event attracted one thousand attendees, and three hundred people made a profession of faith! The next year, the event attracted three thousand students, with another one thousand watching online all over the nation and the world, and five hundred people were saved. It's amazing what God will do when we get bigness in our hearts.

> **It's amazing what God will do when we get bigness in our hearts.**

"'My thoughts are nothing like your thoughts,' says the LORD. 'And my ways are far beyond anything you could imagine. For just as the heavens are higher than the earth, so my ways are higher than your ways and my thoughts higher than your thoughts'" (Isa. 55:8–9 NLT).

You have something to offer the world, something you possess that is dying to come out. It's time to take the limits off your possibilities and begin to see the full size and scope of what is possible in the eyes of God.

God is waiting for you to think big, then think bigger.

Earlier in this chapter, I listed five questions that will help you learn how to think bigger. Write an answer for each of these questions. As with the last action step, don't spend a lot of time analyzing and critiquing your answers. This is a time to think big, then think bigger.

1. If you had all the money in the world, what would you do?

2. If you had all the time in the world, what would you do?

3. If you could talk to the most successful person in your field of interest (dead or alive), what do you suppose his or her advice to you would be?

4. If you knew you couldn't fail, what would you attempt for God?

5. What do you secretly want that you are too embarrassed to tell anyone about?

3

Transform Your Dreams
INTO GOALS

• • • • •

You have a God-given dream. Now, what are you going to do to bring it to pass? A good place to start is with goal setting.

Are you groaning and rolling your eyes right now? Did you consider skipping this chapter just based on the title? If you did, you're in good company. Goal setting is a topic that's been talked and written about so much that we tend to dismiss it out of hand. And that's the problem.

Have you ever heard the adage "Familiarity breeds contempt"? Most of us have heard so much about the importance of goal setting that we tend to look on the idea with contempt. "Been there, done that," we say. That can be a costly mistake.

In his bestselling book, *What They Don't Teach You at Harvard Business School*, Mark H. McCormack tells about a Harvard Business School study conducted between 1979 and 1989. Members of the 1979 graduating class of the Harvard MBA program were asked if they had written down clear goals and made plans to accomplish them. Ten years later, the school conducted a follow-up survey of those same graduates. The study reported some significant results.

> Only 3 percent of the graduates had written goals and plans. Thirteen percent had goals, but they were not in writing. Eighty-four percent had no goals at all other than to enjoy their summer as school was letting out. In 1989, they re-interviewed those graduates, and the findings were staggering: The 13 percent of the graduates who had goals were earning twice the amount of money as those with no goals. Furthermore, another incredible fact emerged: The 3 percent of graduates with clear, written-down goals were earning more than the 97 percent of all the graduates combined![1]

Take a few seconds to let that paragraph sink in. Read it again if you have to. The 3 percent of graduates who had taken the time to write down their goals were earning more than the 97 percent who didn't—*combined*.

I don't know about you, but when I read those statistics, I'm impressed. You see, there's a reason motivational writers and speakers talk so much about goal setting. It works. Why? Time management is life management, and setting goals is foundational to that process. One of the biggest lessons I've learned from seeing my dreams fulfilled is this: what I focus on increases.

> **One of the biggest lessons I've learned from seeing my dreams fulfilled is this: what I focus on increases.**

If I want a closer walk with God, I need to spend more time with him. If I want a better family life, I should plan to spend time with my family. If I want a stronger career, I must focus my attention on whatever is essential to my career success. Whatever our dreams involve, if we want to achieve them, we must focus on what it's going to take to make them a reality. For example, if you are in sales and you want to double your income, you should double the time you spend in front of prospective buyers.

Are you old enough to remember overhead projectors? If the projector cast a blurry image on the screen, you didn't think something was wrong with it and throw it away. You focused it.

Likewise, if your plans are "fuzzy," there's nothing wrong with you; you just need better focus. And that's where goals come in. Think of a goal as a powerful lens that will enable you to bring your dream into sharp focus. Goals are an essential element in accomplishing your God-given dream.

Take a moment to consider the following statement by the apostle Paul, an early Christian leader who wrote nearly half of the New Testament. In a letter to a church, he wrote, "One thing I do: Forgetting what is behind and straining toward what is ahead, I press on toward the goal to win the prize for which God has called me heavenward in Christ Jesus" (Phil. 3:13–14).

Is it any wonder this guy won almost half the world to Christ? Keep in mind he did not have email, a computer, a television ministry, or mass printing. What he had was a clear goal: to win everyone he could to Christ.

Paul had a clearly defined goal, and so should we. But we don't want to set goals for goals' sake. We want our goals to work in harmony with our God-given dreams, just as Paul's did. How do we do that? An Old Testament biblical writer named Joel points us in the right direction.

Joel's short book speaks of how God is the giver of dreams:

> Then, after doing all those things,
>   I will pour out my Spirit upon all people.
> Your sons and daughters will prophesy.
>   Your old men will dream dreams,
>   and your young men will see visions.
> In those days I will pour out my Spirit
>   even on servants—men and women alike. (2:28–29 NLT)

As you begin to think about transforming your dream into goals, take note of a four-step process found in the book of Joel.

First, Look at What God Has Already Done in Your Life

"Then, after doing all those things . . ." (Joel 2:28 NLT).

God has already been at work in your life. His fingerprints are all over your past. Often, if we'll take the time to look at our past, God will give us glimpses of our future.

For example, before the nation of Israel entered the Promised Land, a man named Caleb was chosen to be one of the twelve men sent to check out the land. Even though it would be forty years before Caleb would actually "move in," God allowed him to see the land he was going to give him. In Caleb's case, this was a positive moment, when he saw his future.

> **If we'll take the time to look at our past, God will give us glimpses of our future.**

But God works through negative moments too. Consider Caleb's leader, Moses. Moses grew up in Egypt, in the palace, as Pharaoh's adopted grandson. He had everything going for him, but one day he saw an Egyptian beating one of his fellow Israelites. In one regrettable moment, Moses did the unthinkable. He killed the Egyptian and hid his body in the sand. Even though Moses's act was sinful, underneath his sin was a healthy desire: to set another man free from oppression. Moses wanted to be the one to set his nation free from slavery. It would be many years before God would use Moses to accomplish that very task, but Moses's action revealed the passion of his heart.

Both of these events are examples of what I call a preview. Where has God moved powerfully in your life before? If you take the time to look back on what God has done in your past, you may see a Caleb or a Moses moment, a preview of your coming attractions—your dreams.

Second, Expect God to Stir in You Powerfully

"I will pour out my Spirit upon all people" (Joel 2:28 NLT).

One of the best ways to know your dream is in line with God's will is that it will often come to your mind when you're praying, reading his Word, hearing a message from your pastor or teacher, or even as you read a Christian book (like this one). When God stirs in you, he will draw out your emotions. We are emotional beings, and God can use your emotions to lead you into his will for your life.

Here's a great way to discover the clear dream God is giving you. Answer the following questions: What evokes strong emotion in you? What makes you pound a table in anger or cry your eyes out? What is it that makes you want to take immediate action? Some people call it a "burden," but "passion" is a better description.

As you pray and seek the Lord, you will discover your passion. Before God puts you in motion, he gives you strong emotion. This feeling stirs you and will keep you going when your dream seems unreachable or impossible. Without these emotionally filled spiritual moments, we would probably quit short of our dreams when things became difficult. Imagine what might have happened if Moses didn't have his experience at the burning bush to keep him going when Pharaoh repeatedly said no to his request to let God's people go. Never discount your emotions.

However, I should add one caveat. Emotions and feelings can be wrong. Therefore, you shouldn't trust them blindly without seeking other confirmation. They can also be fleeting and change on a whim. One indication your feelings are from the Lord is that they will be consistent over your lifetime, not just momentary. In addition, they will not be in conflict with what God's Word teaches. Check to make sure your emotions are not violating the Bible, and make yourself accountable to other godly people. I recommend you talk with a pastor or mature believer who is farther along in their walk with God than you are. The book of Proverbs gives solid advice in this regard when it says, "Plans are established by counsel; by wise guidance wage war" (20:18 ESV).

Third, Speak Your Dream Aloud

"Your sons and daughters will prophesy. Your old men will dream dreams, and your young men will see visions" (Joel 2:28 NLT).

Children have an innate ability and innocence that enable them not only to have bold dreams but also to proclaim them without embarrassment. Somewhere along the way, most of us lose the ability to speak our dreams. We do not abandon the dreams; we just become more cautious about sharing them.

Maybe when you were a child you believed you would be an astronaut or professional baseball player. Later you discovered that you didn't possess the abilities to do those things. With age, we learn to assess our skills and talents more accurately. Thus, we must sometimes set aside some of our childhood dreams. Nevertheless, as we get older, the child inside us still needs to dream.

When David was a boy, a prophet told him he would be king. When David was a grown man and King Saul was trying to kill him, David had to remember God's promise for his future. In other words, inside every little boy is a king waiting to come out, and inside every man is a boy still dreaming. This goes for little girls and women too. The passage from Joel says, "Your sons *and daughters.*"

At some point, you have to embrace the dream still inside you. The best way to make your dream come alive again is for you to say it aloud. When you do this, you give it life by making it tangible. There is power in your words. Say them as you write them. Don't worry about what others may think.

An even better way to give form to your dream is to thank God audibly in prayer. Such a prayer may sound something like this: "Thank you, God, for the dream you've given me to go back to school, get my law degree, and become an attorney. I may be thirty-five, but I still have a dream. When I earn my law degree, I will glorify you with it. I will help the hurting, the victim, and all those who need justice."

Whatever your dream is, speak it aloud.

Fourth, Visualize Your Dream as if It's Already a Reality and Write It Down

"Your old men will dream dreams, and your young men will see visions" (Joel 2:28 NLT).

There is no age requirement. Young or old, we all have dreams that God has put inside us. Some of us will dream new dreams as we get older too. The last part of this verse says we will "see visions." A vision combines a mental picture with strong emotions. If you have to add emotion to your dream (in other words, if it takes work to get excited about it), then you may be trying to embrace someone else's dream. Your dream will naturally have strong emotions attached to it because God put it in you. These emotions make you unstoppable.

The way to make your dream come alive is by using your imagination to create a mental picture. Ephesians 3:20 uses the word *imagine*: "Now to him who is able to do immeasurably more than all we ask or imagine, according to his power that is at work within us." No matter how much you can imagine, God can do immeasurably more. You may be limited; he is not.

> No matter how much you can imagine, God can do immeasurably more.

Your imagination is critical to discovering your dream. Paint a picture in your mind by using your imagination. Imagine being the boss. Imagine leading your organization. Imagine running staff meetings and making decisions that grow the company and lead to greater opportunities. Imagine opening a clinic in a remote village. Imagine meeting the needs of children and families who lack good health care and the education necessary to advance in life.

When you paint your mental picture, make sure it's in vivid color and has plenty of detail. As you imagine your dream becoming a reality, feel the emotions that accompany your newfound success.

Once you have visualized your dream, write it down. Why? Writing down your dream makes it concrete. It is now solid and tangible, not just an idea in your head but something you can hold before your eyes. Read over your dream every day and thank God for it. You now have a reason to get up in the morning. You have purpose.

Five Steps to Transform Your Dreams into Goals

Now that you have identified your dream, it's time to transform it into achievable goals. And even if your dream is huge, transforming it into goals you can reach is easier than you may think.

Be Specific

When you set a goal, don't say, "I want to become successful." What does success look like for you?

For example, here's what success looks like for me. I want to lead and pastor a growing church that reaches very specific goals in critical areas. The number of people saved in a year, how many churches we help start, and how much money we are able to give to missions are all metrics I care about.

Regarding your own goals, you might say, "I want to earn over one hundred thousand dollars a year by the time I'm forty." Or "I want to enroll in a degree program and complete at least two courses by this time next year."

Make Your Goals Measurable

If you can't measure your goals, you can't manage them. Saying you want to be a good parent sounds great, but it's too general. What does a good parent look like? How much time are you going to spend with your kids each week? Each day? Does good parenting involve taking the family on vacations? How often and for how long?

Maybe you want to be a millionaire. Does that mean you want a million dollars in the bank or a million dollars in real estate assets? How will you get there, and how long will it take?

Maybe you want to be closer to God. What does that look like? Does it involve Bible study and personal devotions? How often and for how long? You can measure quantity, but you can also measure quality. How do you know you are close to God? For me, I want to feel his pleasure as I do his work. For you, a close walk with God may look different.

Set Deadlines

For me, setting deadlines is the hardest part of goal setting. I'm facing a deadline right now as I write this book. Even though most of us don't like deadlines, they are great motivators. Without them, we don't have a goal; we have a wish.

When you set deadlines, challenge yourself, but be realistic. Rick Warren, pastor and author of *The Purpose Driven Life*, says, "We overestimate what we can do in a year and underestimate what we can do in a lifetime."[2] A way to keep your goals big but reachable is to break them down into smaller units. Try setting long-term deadlines for your major goals, and then break them down into intermediate and short-term goals.

And don't just think about a deadline for finishing. You may need to set a deadline for starting a project. For example, if your goal is to get your GED, you might write down something like, "I am going to enroll in my local community college GED program at least six weeks before the fall semester." I find my most important deadline is not when I will finish but when I will start.

Deadlines force you to move beyond dreaming and actually do something about your dreams.

Schedule Your Goals

Once you've written down your goals and deadlines, put them on your calendar. It doesn't matter whether you use a paper or digital calendar. Put the deadlines down wherever you'll be reminded of them regularly. Digital calendars are great for this, because you can set them to send you reminders via email or text messaging.

If you don't use a digital calendar, you might consider buying a wall calendar that enables you to look at a whole year at one time. If you do this, put it up in a place where you'll see it several times a day. The bathroom and kitchen are good locations.

If none of these options works for you, then use a notebook-style appointment calendar. However, if you use a notebook, develop a habit of reviewing your goals, subgoals, and deadlines regularly—every day, if you can.

Create a To-Do List

Now that your deadlines are on your calendar, it's time to create a to-do list based on those deadlines. This is a critical step in transforming a dream into a reachable goal. For example, you may have set a goal to drop thirty pounds in five months. Although weight loss might not qualify as a life dream, it's a good example of how to work toward a major goal by subgoals. It's specific, measurable, and reachable. The problem is that you still have to figure out how you're going to achieve that goal. In other words, you need an action plan. That's where to-do lists come in.

First, you need to figure out a reasonable amount of weight to lose each week. Most health experts recommend no more than two pounds per week. Therefore, you schedule a subgoal of losing one to two pounds this week. But even that isn't enough. *How* do you plan to lose those pounds? You're probably going to need to plan some exercise sessions this week, and you may want to consider a change of diet.

How to Turbocharge Your Goals

Do you want to reach your goals more quickly? Turbo-charge them by increasing your efforts and shrinking the rest period between efforts. Rest is important, but most of us are not overworked.

One technique I use to turbo-charge my goals is to "accordion" them. As a small child, I used to make a fan or an accordion by folding a sheet of paper back and forth into small pleats. You can do something like this with your deadlines. You "accordion" your deadlines by squeezing them closer together and intensifying your efforts. For example, this year my goal has shifted from writing one book to writing three in one year. However, to make this happen, I will have to intensify my efforts. If I've been writing one thousand words a day, I'll need to write three thousand words a day. To write those additional two thousand words, I'll have to carve out extra writing time each day.

Many of our goals are long term, but if we're honest, we've allowed ourselves way too much time to accomplish them. Maybe you have a goal to buy one rental house a year for the next ten years. What if you "accordion" your goal and buy one rental house every six months? It is possible. I know a man who bought eleven properties in twelve months.

You may be thinking, *This all sounds great, but I just don't have time to add new goals, and I certainly don't have time to turbo-charge them.* In reality, you have a lot more time than you think. When you're transforming dreams into goals, it's important to take a long look at how you are using your time.

> **One of the best ways to accomplish something great in your life is not by adding but by subtracting.**

One of the best ways to accomplish something great in your life is not by adding but by subtracting. What are the time wasters in your life? Is there some activity you could drop in order to find the time you need to make and reach your goals? I challenge you to turn off the television set or the internet for a week and see how much extra time you have.

Every year I try to make a not-to-do list. I identify the time wasters in my life and make a concerted effort to stop doing those things. This helps me focus on what matters most to me. We don't need more time; we need better priorities.

Don't Quit

The most important aspect of goal setting is sticking to your goals. In other words, don't quit. As you begin to work toward your goals, setbacks will happen. The proper response to a setback is always the same. Pick up where you left off. Never give up on your goals. To give up on your life goals is to give up on your life.

In his classic book *Think and Grow Rich*, Napoleon Hill tells about a man who went to Colorado during the gold rush, staked a claim, and began digging. He had a very specific, tangible, and focused goal. And after a few weeks of hard work, he struck gold. He immediately went home and raised the money for the equipment he would need to mine the vein. Initial results indicated that he had found one of the richest mines in Colorado. Sadly, the mine played out, and he got discouraged. He sold all his equipment and went home. But the man who bought his equipment didn't give up. He did some research, went back to the mine, and began drilling. As it turned out, the first miner had stopped drilling just three feet short of a vein that would ultimately yield millions of dollars' worth of gold ore.[3]

> If you get discouraged and quit when you face difficulties and challenges, you may be stopping just short of the exciting blessings God has for you.

God did not put dreams in your heart to frustrate you but rather to fulfill you. If you get discouraged and quit when you face difficulties and challenges, you may be stopping just short of the exciting blessings God has for you.

Recently, I had the privilege of traveling to Dachau, Germany, to visit the infamous concentration camp where many Jews and political dissidents were enslaved, tortured, and killed. As I walked around the camp, I kept thinking how terrible it must have been to be imprisoned and have your liberty—and your life—taken from you. All I could think about was how thankful I was to have the freedom to live my life.

What are you and I doing with our freedom? We need to live life to the fullest. Dream big, set goals, and work toward those goals every day.

Find a quiet place and write one of your God-given dreams. Now take the time to think through the steps or subgoals you'll need to fulfill that dream. If you're not sure what those subgoals should be, try asking yourself, *What is the next thing I have to do to accomplish this dream?* Write that down, then ask yourself what the next step would be. Keep repeating that process until you have listed all the steps you need to take to accomplish your dream.

4

CHANGE
Your Beliefs

• • • • •

Many of us live lives of contradiction. On the one hand, we claim to believe God is all-powerful, that nothing is impossible for him. For example, we believe Jesus rose from the dead and is coming again. We believe he can save us from our sins. But when we get down to the nitty-gritty of our personal lives, we don't believe God can or will do anything great in us.

Can you relate?

The Bible clearly states that we have the same power working in us that Christ had. Paul told the Roman Christians, "The Spirit of God, who raised Jesus from the dead, lives in you" (Rom. 8:11 NLT). Isn't that amazing? If we believe in Jesus Christ, the Holy Spirit—the same person who resurrected Jesus—is living in us. If that's true, why do we believe God can do so little in our lives?

In the preceding chapters, we explored our God-given dreams and set goals based on those dreams. The next step is to believe that, with God's help, we can see those dreams fulfilled, far beyond anything we could have imagined.

I have a conviction that changed my life, and it can change yours too. I believe that God put everything and everyone around me to help me become what he wants me to be. Have you ever heard the Bible verse, "And we know that for those who love God all things work together for good, for those who are called according to his purpose" (Rom. 8:28 ESV)? Most of the time, we apply that verse to trials or tragedies, but if you read it closely, you will notice it says "all things." That means God is working in every circumstance I face and through every person I encounter, and his purpose is to bring about good.

This does not mean we blindly trust everyone, and it is not a promise that our lives are going to be easy. However, it does mean we have all we need to accomplish everything God wants us to do with our lives. Simon Peter, one of Jesus's disciples, wrote, "[God's] divine power has given us everything we need for a godly life through our knowledge of him who called us by his own glory and goodness" (2 Pet. 1:3). If we really believed God has given us everything we need to accomplish his will, how would that change our thinking? And if our thinking changed, how would it affect our actions?

> **If we really believed God has given us everything we need to accomplish his will, how would that change our thinking?**

What you believe will have an influence on what you do.

You Are What You Believe

There is an adage that states, "You aren't what you think you are, but what you think, you are." People who do great things believe they can. If you want to accomplish what God wants you to accomplish, if you want to fulfill your purpose, then you must believe that you are able.

I struggled all the way through school. In fact, I frequently had to take remedial classes just to advance to the next grade. I'll never forget sitting in the hallway outside my third-grade classroom, working on a math worksheet I couldn't understand while the rest of my class moved on to another subject. My teacher grew frustrated as she went over the math worksheet with me time and again. She asked me repeatedly, "Now do you understand?" By the fourth and fifth grade, I learned how to fake it. I nodded like I understood. I would work on my paper until the entire class was finished. When it was time to turn in our papers, I would quickly fill in the last half with guesses and hand it over to the teacher.

That was bad enough, but then came high school. Truth be told, two or three of my high school friends should have a share of my diploma, because they are the only reason I graduated. I could ask them for help, and they would put up with me longer than my teachers would.

Years later my wife asked me what I learned in public school. I told her I learned that I was dumb. It wasn't until my last few years of college that I found something I showed promise in— speech communications. Suddenly, the final exams were not tests but speeches. I went from Cs and Ds to As and Bs overnight.

Everyone feels confident about something. For some of my friends, it was

> **If you want to accomplish what God wants you to accomplish, if you want to fulfill your dreams, then you must believe that you are able.**

football, and for others, it was schoolwork. For me, it happened when I stepped onto a stage and spoke to a room full of people. I call this the place of instant confidence. You are in the place of instant confidence not just when you're good at something but when you *know* and *believe* you're good at it.

When I was a child, my mother always told me, "Billy, God's hand is on your life. You are going to do great things for God one day." Her words helped me through the times when I lacked confidence in school. Because of what she said, I developed an inner belief that I was going to do great things one day. The right belief can carry you through incredibly difficult times. On the other hand, the wrong belief can stop you cold, even if everything else is in your favor.

For years, most psychological researchers focused on abnormal and unhealthy behavior. But at the turn of the twentieth century, a psychologist named William James changed this. James wrote, "There is a law in psychology that if you form a picture in your mind of what you would like to be, and you keep and hold that picture there long enough, you will soon become exactly as you have been thinking."[1]

James's findings have been scrutinized and questioned, yet his findings have stood the test of time. The Bible affirms a similar principle: "As a man thinks in his heart, so is he" (Prov. 23:7).

What you believe shapes how you perceive the world around you. If you believe that today will be a good day, you will probably have a good day. If you start out thinking it is going to be a bad day, that will probably be your experience. Thankfully, you can choose your attitudes and beliefs. And if you've been living with negative ones, you can change them.

Change Your Beliefs

Imagine there was a Belief Store just down the road. If you could go to a store and buy beliefs and attitudes, which ones would you purchase? Maybe, like me, you would buy a belief that would change your academic career: "I am smart." Maybe your belief would be, "I am good with money." Or how about, "I am attractive and fun to be around"? That one would help tremendously if you are single and shy. A belief I continuously recommend for others to adopt (and one of my personal favorites) is, "With God's help, I can do this" (see Phil. 4:13).

Of course, you won't find a Belief Store just down the road. But you don't need one. Beliefs are all free of charge. You can believe whatever you want to believe, and it won't cost you a penny.

Now, before you think I've gone off the deep end, I'm not saying that believing something automatically makes it true. You can believe that space aliens make crop circles and that the Loch Ness monster exists, but that doesn't make those things a reality.

I'm not talking about that kind of believing. I'm talking about what you believe about yourself, your abilities, and your relationship to God. I teach people that God wants to bless them, and sometimes those people disagree with me. I just respond, "Believe what you want to believe. I choose to believe what the Bible says, and it says that God loves me and will bless me." This doesn't mean I won't face challenges or tragedies, but it does mean I have God's power to help me in my weakness. "My grace is sufficient for you, for my power is made perfect in weakness" (2 Cor. 12:9 ESV).

Replace Negative Attitudes with Positive Affirmations

There is one other caveat when it comes to the Belief Store. While all beliefs are free up front, and you can choose whichever ones you want, the beliefs you embrace can cost you something in the long term. In his book *Illusions*, Richard Bach writes, "Argue for your limitations and sure enough, they're yours."[2] For example, if you adopt the conviction "I don't deserve to be happy," that belief may cause you to run from anyone or anything that might make you happy. If you tell yourself, "I'm not good with money," then you may never open your mind to learning how to handle money and investments.

In his book *Change Your Thinking, Change Your Life*, Brian Tracy describes the power of belief this way: "You do not believe what you see. Rather, you see what you *already* believe. You can have life-enhancing beliefs that make you happy and optimistic, or you can have negative beliefs about yourself and your potential that act as roadblocks to the realization of everything that is truly possible for you."[3]

> A key step in achieving your dreams is to stop believing why you can't do something and start believing why you can.

A key step in achieving your dreams is to stop believing why you can't do something and start believing why you can. It's time to doubt your doubts. You are in charge of your own mind. Take control of those negative, self-limiting attitudes and embrace what God says about you. "But in all these things we are completely victorious through God who showed his love for us" (Rom. 8:37 NCV). God says you are a winner. You are an overcomer. You are a champion. You are a child of the King. It's time to believe it so that you will begin to act like it.

John Maxwell says that you cannot act in a way inconsistent with how you feel about yourself.[4] Change your beliefs about yourself, and you will change how you act. Change your beliefs about your job, and your career will improve. Change your beliefs about God, and you will sense his power in your life!

Make Sure Your Words Match Your Beliefs

People often ask me questions after I give a talk at church or at a conference. Someone will walk up and say, "Will you pray for me? I just can't overcome this problem."

I have learned to stop them in their tracks and tell them that their mouth gave them away. I say, "You just said, 'I can't.' I want you never to say that unbiblical lie from the pit of hell again." I then tell them that by changing their language they can change their belief, and ultimately their life. I say, "From now on say, 'I haven't done this yet, but I will.'"

Maybe you have been saying, "I just can't find the right person for me." Instead, tell yourself, "I'm single, and I believe God has someone for me just around the corner." Instead of saying, "I can't seem to get ahead financially," tell yourself, "I know God has a money-making idea just for me. I know my finances are about to change!" There is a miracle in your mouth. Make sure your words match your new belief.

In Revelation 22:16, Jesus refers to himself as the "bright Morning Star." This means he is the sun rising in the morning. He is your new day. As we conclude this chapter, I challenge you to believe this is a new day for you. All the messes from your past are behind you. You cannot change yesterday, but your today is already changing. "See, I am doing a new thing! Now it springs up; do you not perceive it?" (Isa. 43:19).

Believe that today is a new day, a new opportunity. This is your opportunity to walk with God in confidence because he forgives you of all sin. "But if we confess our sins to him, he is faithful and just to forgive us our sins and to cleanse us from all wickedness" (1 John 1:9 NLT). Today you can make a fresh start in your marriage, your career, your parenting, your faith, your finances, and anything else you want to believe God for.

Do you believe it?

Choose to!

I've discovered that if I don't believe I can change something in my life, then I won't even try to change it. But when my beliefs change, so do my behavior and my expectations.

Write a wrong belief that has been holding you back. Then, next to it, write down a new belief to replace the old belief. Here are a few examples:

Old Belief	New Belief
I'm only happy if I can eat fried chicken.	Nothing I can eat will taste as good as I'll feel from eating healthy.
I'm not good with money, and I'll always be broke.	I'm good with money, and money ideas are constantly flowing my way.
I always mess things up.	With God's help, I can handle this!

5

Cover Your Dreams
WITH PRAYER

• • • • •

Almost a decade ago, I found myself at the point of exhaustion. Too many responsibilities and not enough time were taking their toll. I spoke with our church leaders and decided to take a much-needed vacation. Jessica and I decided to go to Walt Disney World in Orlando, Florida, without the kids. (Before you give me the "Worst Dad of the Year Award," I want you to know I've taken my children there also, just not this particular time.)

While we were at Disney World, I was amazed at the large and well-run Disney organization. Wandering through the huge amusement park, we stumbled upon an attraction called "Walt's Dream" located inside Disney's Hollywood Studios. I love to read and study the stories of successful entrepreneurs, so there was no way I was going to miss the opportunity to walk through an exhibit covering the life and history of Walt Disney.

At the end of the exhibit, we watched a twenty-minute film featuring Walt himself. The film covered how Walt got the idea for Mickey Mouse as well as the creation and subsequent success of the film company and theme parks. I was inspired, but I wasn't prepared for what happened next. At the end of the movie, Walt Disney said, "I only hope that we never lose sight of one thing—that it was all started by a mouse."

When I heard those words, I sensed God saying, "If a man can build all of this with a mouse, what can you do with the Holy Spirit?"

While everyone else exited the theater, I just sat there, stunned. My wife looked at me and said, "Are you okay?" She saw the expression on my face and knew something had changed inside me. Then she said, "We're not starting another church, are we?"

I laughed. "Don't worry," I replied. "That's not what God is telling me, but he is talking to me."

She said, "Why don't you take the next few days to pray and ask God what he is trying to tell you?"

As we walked around the parks, I prayed under my breath, "God, what is the next step for our church? What is your vision for our church?"

I thought if Walt Disney were still alive, he would be amazed at how big his dream of a family entertainment company had become. I began to ask God to show me how big his dream was for his church. What would be possible if God had his way?

Over the next few days, I sensed God saying, "Pray more." I responded, "Okay, God, I'll do that." Then I would pray more as we continued to enjoy Disney World.

On the last day of our vacation, I began to press God for clear direction. "Lord, I'm praying, and you keep telling me to pray more. How much more? Five hours? Ten hours?" As I began to ask God to quantify my prayer time, we rounded a corner, and right in front of me was a giant sign attached to the Epcot ball with the number one hundred on it. The sign was in honor of Walt Disney's one hundredth birthday, but God used that number for something different for me.

I sensed God might be telling me to pray for one hundred hours about the next chapter of our ministry. I told Jessica what I thought God might be leading me to do. She said, "What could it hurt to pray for one hundred hours?" I agreed it certainly couldn't hurt, and it definitely would help.

On our way home, I made a commitment to pray for one hundred hours for the express purpose of hearing from God about his vision for our church. When I got home, I told the church during our weekend services that God was leading me to pray for one hundred hours and asked every individual in the congregation to help hold me to it. I quickly learned they were happy to do so.

The Mechanics of One Hundred Hours of Prayer

So how, exactly, does one pray for one hundred hours?

My tools were a Bible, a pen, a notebook, and the stopwatch on my digital watch. I took two sheets of paper from the organizer I carry around with me and wrote down the numbers 1 to 100. Then I started the timer and began to pray.

My plan was to pray in one-hour sessions. As I prayed, if my mind wandered, I would immediately stop the timer, get focused back on prayer, and then start it again. (This happened a lot, because I have a touch of Attention Deficit Disorder.) At the end of each hour, as the time expired, a buzzer would go off on my watch. Whatever I was thinking about as the buzzer sounded I would write down next to that hour on my organizer page.

You'd be amazed at how a theme begins to develop over the course of one hundred hours, but it didn't start out that way. From hours one to ten, I prayed about everything I could think of. I prayed for myself, my marriage, my kids, the ministry, our small groups, our outreach opportunities, the youth group, and so on. I prayed for world peace, our city leaders, the president of the United States, and better weather. You name it, I prayed for it.

And nothing happened.

I was at home alone for hour ten because it was my day off. In frustration, I went into my bedroom and yelled at God. "God, you got me into this mess. People are expecting me to hear from you, and you haven't told me anything. I don't know what else to pray about!"

That's when it happened. God spoke. He waited until I ran out of things to pray about. Then he said, "Are you done?" I sensed him telling me, "Now that you are done talking, I want you to learn to listen to me." I began to weep. I told him how sorry I was because I thought prayer meant talking to him, but I was not giving him a chance to talk to me.

You see, in my arrogance, I believed I was going to convince God to do something big on my behalf. I spent the first ten hours trying to tell God to do something big. He used the next ninety hours to show me he was already doing something bigger.

Your Misery Becomes Your Ministry

Before I tell you what happened next, I need to give you a bit of background.

When Jessica and I planted our church, we did not have much help. We received some funding from a handful of churches and the denomination I grew up in, but that was it. I also did not have access to good training, so I had to get it where I could find it, and that proved difficult. In other words, we were broke and felt very alone those first few years, but we just kept pressing forward, believing in God for greater things. But to be perfectly honest, we would have been so thankful if someone had come alongside us, not only to assist us but also to guide us through the process.

During my one-hundred-hour prayer time, I began to sense that God was going to give us a ministry to help other pastors who were trying to start churches. In other words, our misery was about to become our ministry.

At around hour fifty, something happened that is difficult to explain. I had a dream, but it didn't occur while I was asleep. While I was praying, I saw people from all over the world walking up to me. As they approached, they were all speaking to me in their own languages, but I was hearing them in mine. It was like a reverse-Pentecost moment. They were all saying, "When are you going to start the church for me? When are you going to start the church that will reach my family?"

I sensed the Spirit of God come over me as I never had before, and I knew in that moment that God had called me to plant one hundred churches around the world. Even as I am writing this, tears are coming to my eyes because I'm so thankful God spoke to me in that moment.

The next fifty hours were all about the details of how we would go about planting a crop of next-generation churches all over the world. I knew that to have the base of support we would need to be able to give a million dollars annually to see this vision implemented, our church would need to grow to over ten thousand people.

So what was my takeaway after one hundred hours of praying? One of the biggest discoveries I made was that I used to pray to discover God's will. What I learned was that praying to God *is his will*.

Another takeaway was a clear vision and call from God. I sent out an advertising piece inviting all members and attendees to "come hear what God showed Pastor Bil Cornelius in one hundred hours of prayer."

> **I used to pray to discover God's will. What I learned was that praying to God *is his will*.**

The place was packed!

I told them the same story I just told you and explained that our church was going to plant one hundred churches worldwide while training pastors and their churches how to do the same. Our people responded with enthusiastic standing ovations at every service because they felt filled with God's purpose.

A side benefit that I did not expect was that I suddenly began to have spiritual authority. For example, most leaders struggle at one time or another with people who question their vision. After this experience, when someone would say, "I don't agree with your vision," I would respond humbly, yet confidently, "I prayed about this for one hundred hours. How long have you prayed?"

Don't misunderstand me. My answer was not about one-upping someone or having a clever put-down. It was simply a way of communicating to people that I had sincerely sought God and was doing what he had led me to do. After my one hundred hours of prayer, I understood why Moses could confidently approach Pharaoh and demand that the people of Israel be set free. Moses had heard directly from God. The reason Peter could go almost overnight from denying Christ to being the bold leader of the rapidly expanding church in Jerusalem was that he had been with Jesus.

When we seek God, he speaks to us. He wants to speak to you, to give you his vision for your life. But as you seek him, he will go one step further than just giving you his vision for your life. He will give you his power.

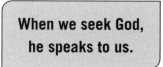

When we seek God, he speaks to us.

Through this prayer experience, I painstakingly learned three key steps to follow in approaching or seeking God.

Step 1

Practice the Presence of God

Approach your prayer time as something that you start and God finishes. Take your Bible, a pen, and a notebook with you and, as he leads, read until he speaks to you. Ask questions. "God, are you telling me this?" Continue reading and write out your thoughts in your notebook.

I recommend you get a one-year Bible or use a reading plan that takes you through the entire Bible in a year or two. I can't even begin to tell you how many times I would write down a question I had for God and then have the Lord directly answer my question through that day's reading.

Step 2

Receive His Direction and Power

When you sense God speaking to you, write down what you think he's telling you. Make sure it aligns with Scripture. But most importantly, don't get up too quickly. Stay and pray longer. Ask more questions and push through. God begins to pour on his presence when you wait for him.

Very few people will wait. But if you do, God will honor your perseverance. "Those who hope in the LORD will renew their strength" (Isa. 40:31). As you wait on God, you will find your mind flooded with new ideas from him. However, many times these ideas will only be seeds. After God gives you an idea, ask him to give you the steps you need to take. Then flesh them out on paper.

Step 3

Seek Confirmation

After you have written down your idea, ask God for confirmation. If the idea is from him, he will confirm it in your heart. One of the ways you can know that God is speaking to you is that he will lead you to do what seems impossible. Jesus told his disciples, "What is impossible for people is possible with God" (Luke 18:27 NLT).

> One of the ways you can know that God is speaking to you is that he will lead you to do what seems impossible.

God also confirms his direction through the counsel and advice of godly people. The bigger the decision you are making, the more intensely you should seek confirmation not only from God but also from people who are walking closely with the Lord. God spoke to Moses through a burning bush. But Moses also received advice from his father-in-law, Jethro (see Exod. 18:13–24).

Why is seeking God in prayer so important? God has a secret to share with you. He won't let anyone else in on this secret except you. Secrets create real intimacy. I have intimacy with my wife because there are things we know about each other that no one else will ever know. God wants it that way with you. He has a secret to tell you that you can only learn when you are in his presence long enough to hear it. You must be broken and open. When you are, then he will tell you the biggest secret he has for you. He will tell you who you really are, what you can really do, and what you can truly have. When you discover this, you will finally begin to know just how amazing God is.

He will challenge you to grow by giving you a God-sized dream that demands a life of faith. And as you move forward to see those dreams fulfilled, God's presence will go with you and will keep you calm in the midst of impossible odds as you trust and obey him. Remember, Jesus said, "What is impossible for people is possible with God" (Luke 18:27 NLT).

I would like to challenge you to lay your dreams before God and cover them with prayer. God may not lead you to pray for one hundred hours. Could you commit to praying for five hours? Or ten? Fifteen? There's no magic number of hours to pray. The key is being willing to keep at it until you hear from God.

The only tools you need are:

- Bible
- notebook
- pen or pencil
- stopwatch or timer
- a quiet, comfortable place where you won't be disturbed

Write down in your notebook your commitment to pray. It may look something like this: "By faith, I am committing to pray for _____ hours about (write down your dream). I am going to humble my heart and seek God's will, whatever that may be."

Part 2

EMBRACING
Your God-Given Dreams

6

CULTIVATE
Risk-Taking Faith

• • • • •

God has given you a dream. You have set goals based on that dream and have chosen to believe God for bigger things in your life. Now it's time to do something that most of us hate to do: take a risk. One of the reasons many people never accomplish their dreams is that they're not willing to risk failure. They feel safer with the status quo, even though they are unsatisfied with it. If you are going to obey God's leading and begin to live out your dream, I guarantee doing so will involve risk.

There's a verse in the book of Hebrews that tells us, "Without faith it is impossible to please God" (11:6). The only way to really please God is to step out and take a risk, because that's what faith involves. If you don't believe that, check out the story of Joshua.

"After the death of Moses the LORD's servant, the LORD spoke to Joshua son of Nun, Moses' assistant. He said, 'Moses my servant is dead. Therefore, the time has come for you to lead these people, the Israelites, across the Jordan River into the land I am giving them'" (Josh. 1:1–2 NLT).

Moses's generation had died off, and now Joshua's generation was taking over. Joshua was given a specific dream from God. He was to be Moses's successor, and his task was to lead the Israelites across the Jordan River so they could take possession of the Promised Land. However, there was one problem with the timing of God's command: "It was the harvest season, and the Jordan was overflowing its banks" (Josh. 3:15 NLT). In other words, God told Joshua and the people of Israel to cross the Jordan River at the worst possible time. I imagine some of the people wondered if it wouldn't be better to wait until the waters were lower and the currents not so dangerous.

> **If you are going to obey God's leading and begin to live out your dream, I guarantee doing so will involve risk.**

Have you ever heard someone say, "The safest place to be is in the Lord's will"? This is a nice saying, but based on my experience, God often leads us to do things that are not safe. But such times are often God's opportunity to prove himself.

As you think about your God-given dreams and the goals you have set, are you hesitating to put them into practice because:

- You don't have the money?
- You don't have the time?
- You don't know the right people?
- You are underqualified?
- You are scared?

It's time to step out in faith. I want to challenge you to begin working on your plans and goals today. When God told Joshua to cross the Jordan River, he meant immediately. God didn't give them the option of waiting until the water level dropped. The same is true with us. God does not give us dreams so we can sit around and think about them. If we think too much about our plans, we end up with analysis paralysis. In other words, we think but never act. That is why we need to set deadlines for starting projects, not just finishing them. I once heard a wise man say, "Getting started is the same as being halfway done."

How strange would it be if you went to a shooting range and all the instructor ever let you do was aim your gun at a target? Sooner or later you'd ask, "Don't I ever get to shoot?" But that's exactly what many of us do with our dreams. We think about them. We may even write goals and make plans. But we never take the first step toward achieving them.

> **God often leads us to do things that are not safe. But such times are often God's opportunity to prove himself.**

It's time to stop taking aim and pull the trigger. This means that you finally apply for that job. Or you ask that girl out. Or you send that email, apologize to the one you hurt, confront your spouse, go back to school, ask for the loan, join that church, or do whatever it is that God is telling you to do.

When you only talk about your dreams, the only thing you're putting off is your future. Think about Joshua and the Israelites camped along the shores of the Jordan River. If they stayed where they were, they would never take possession of the land God had promised them. And even though it was the worst possible time, Joshua led them forward with boldness.

Why? Because Joshua had a promise from God. God told him, "Wherever you set foot, you will be on land I have given you. . . . For I will be with you as I was with Moses. I will not fail you or abandon you" (Josh. 1:3, 5 NLT).

Even when you are unsure of yourself, be assured of this: God loves you and believes in you, or he wouldn't have given you your dream. The fact that God gave you the dream means he also gave you everything you need to accomplish it. Every step you take, remember that God is with you. He will guide you and lead you.

If God is speaking to you right now, it's time to move out of mediocrity and start moving in the direction he is leading you.

What If I Fail?

Fear of failure is a major reason why many people never accomplish their goals. They are so worried about falling flat on their faces that they never even try. Never let the fear of failure hold you back.

One day I challenged a single man to ask out a girl he was obviously interested in. He said to me, "What if I ask her out for this Friday night and she says no?"

I said, "Then you'll be right where you are now—alone."

What if you start that business and it fails? Then you'll have a first-rate education on how to start and fail at business. And you'll be better prepared for the next time you try.

The church I started has grown from five to nine thousand people, but this is my second church plant. The first one failed under my leadership. So did I fail? Yes. Am I a failure? No.

Here's an important principle to remember: failure is an event, not a person. Just because you have been unsuccessful at something doesn't mean you are a failure personally. In fact, the average successful millionaire entrepreneur starts over eleven businesses before making her first million. Wouldn't you say the ten businesses that failed were worth it?

Have you ever seen a baby try to walk and then fall down and give up? No way! The baby keeps getting up and trying until he learns to walk. Likewise, the possibility of failure should never keep you from starting to reach for your goals. If you fall down, just get up and try again. You are not a failure because something doesn't work out; you are a failure when you don't even try. As long as you don't give up, failure is never final.

Be Willing to Get Messy

It would have been easy for Joshua and the Israelites to remain camped out on the east bank of the Jordan. Have you ever seen a river at flood stage? As Joshua and the Israelites stood at the edge of the Jordan River, they saw that the water had overflowed its banks and the current was powerful. This was a huge risk for the priests—the ones who had to lead the way. They could have just said, "You know, it's pretty nice right here. Why don't we just forget about the Promised Land—at least until the water level goes down."

But when they took the risk, look what God did for them: "But as soon as the feet of the priests who were carrying the Ark touched the water at the river's edge, the water above that point began backing up a great distance away. . . . Then all the people crossed over near the town of Jericho" (Josh. 3:15–16 NLT).

Just imagine being a priest and having to carry the ark of the covenant. The ark contained God's presence and his Word. I would not want to be the guy who lost my footing in the water and dropped the ark of the covenant into the river. Can you imagine the pressure?

God performed a miracle on behalf of Joshua, the priests, and the people of God. He stopped the flow of the river and caused the water to back up so that they could cross on dry land. However, the Bible is clear that the miracle did not take place until after the priests had stepped into the water.

> **God wants you to take a step of faith that will be messy before he turns it into a miracle.**

God performed a miracle on behalf of Joshua, the priests, and the people of God, and he will do the same for you. However, God wants you to take a step of faith that will be messy before he turns it into a miracle. Just as the people followed the ark (God's presence and his Word) into the Promised Land, God expects you to follow him into your promised land.

Learn How to "Occupy"

One core principle that has helped me keep moving forward in my life and ministry is the principle of "occupying." When God spoke to Joshua and the Israelites in Deuteronomy 32:47, he said they would occupy the land when they crossed the Jordan River. As I studied what God told Joshua, I noticed that Jesus used "occupy" in the New Testament.

When Jesus was discussing the kingdom of God, he used a parable (a story) to explain how the kingdom works in our everyday lives. He said, "A nobleman was called away to a distant empire to be crowned king and then return. Before he left, he called together ten of his servants and divided among them ten pounds of silver, saying, '*Invest* this for me while I am gone'" (Luke 19:12–13 NLT, emphasis added).

The principle is easy to miss here, until you read the last part of this verse in the King James Version. You see, when the King James Version was translated, to "invest" in something meant something different from what it means to us today. Today the word *invest* conjures up images of stocks, bonds, mutual funds, a CD, or even a business. But in those times, to invest meant that you needed land. Land enabled you, as the investor, to either plant a crop or raise livestock. So a new investment meant you needed to rent or purchase new ground.

This is how the verse reads in the King James Version: "And he called his ten servants, and delivered them ten pounds, and said unto them, '*Occupy* till I come'" (Luke 19:13 KJV, emphasis added). "*Invest* till I come" in the New Living Translation is rendered "*occupy* till I come" in the King James Version.

This insight changed my life. As a pastor, I was trying to expand our outreach, so I was planning to open a second campus. We were already at capacity at our current location, and I was preaching at six services every weekend. We knew it was time to open a second location. I began to study other churches that had opened multiple venues. Some did it by investing millions of dollars and hiring three or four full-time staff members before the doors of the new campus even opened. This was not an option for us. We did not have the money. Then God showed me that sometimes you just have to "occupy."

For us, to occupy meant we had to take a risk and start a new campus by faith. We went to a town forty-five minutes away and rented space by the hour. We then asked a few of our members who lived in that town to join us at the new location. I had no money and no staff, but I had a directive from God. "Just occupy." So we did, and the people came. After that, the people helped provide the money to start a new church.

Did we risk failure? Yes. Did we make mistakes? Lots of them. But sometimes the only way to figure out how to do something is to make mistakes while you're doing it. Someone once told me that anything worth doing is worth doing badly at first. We made plenty of mistakes when we opened our second campus, but because of the principle of "occupying," we now have ten campuses.

Following God Is Always Worth the Risk

You are never more alive than when you are taking risks. Some seek risk artificially. They go to Las Vegas once or twice a year just so they can feel alive. They can't stay awake past 8 p.m. at home but will go to Vegas and gamble all night long. Sadly, they live lives that are boring, mundane, and predictable. God has a better way. It's time to realize that the answer to feeling alive is not in gambling your life savings away but in stepping out in faith and living your dreams.

The average person watches at least four hours of television a day. Rather than watching other people live out their dreams of becoming famous, why don't you invest in (or should I say occupy) your own future? You have the vision and you have the time. I challenge you to quit putting off your future. When you begin by taking a risk, life suddenly becomes interesting.

Step out. Take a risk. Following God is always worth the risk.

Review the dreams and the goals you have set. Which ones are you ready to pursue? This is the time to "occupy," to trust God and act. Keep in mind that stepping out in faith doesn't mean you don't plan. Here are the steps our church followed when we started the second campus.

1. Listen to God. Take the time to hear from God and confirm that you have a God-given dream.

2. Decide to act. Set goals. This is where your faith is activated. You are now putting a demand on your faith.

3. Make a plan. If your decision involves you alone, write your action plan down and keep it in a prominent place. If more than one person is involved, this is the time to get all the key players together and make a plan. If the plan is a long-term plan, break it down into small steps.

4. Set a deadline. A deadline is critical or no one will get started, including you. Set a deadline for getting started, ideally no more than a week from the meeting called in step 3.

5. Set a completion date. How do you know you have "occupied"? For me, it was easy. We would have our first Sunday morning service at the new campus in less than six weeks. This fired up everyone—and scared some—but it got us moving. Set a reasonable date for completing your task.

6. Celebrate when you are standing on the "new ground." When we opened the new location, we celebrated at both locations by announcing the grand opening attendance and also by going to the new location and throwing a party.

Now it's your turn. Choose one of your dreams and "occupy" by following the six steps given above. And remember that the only way to guarantee failure is not to try at all.

7

DEVELOP
the Action Habit

• • • • •

Do you remember the story about Jesus's disciple Peter walking on the water? It's probably one of the most amazing and motivating stories in the New Testament (Matt. 14:22–33). After the feeding of the five thousand, Jesus remained behind and sent the disciples on ahead, across the Sea of Galilee. In the middle of the night, a strong wind came up and kept the boat from making progress. As the disciples were fighting the waves, they saw Jesus coming to them, walking on the lake. They were scared to death and thought he was a ghost. (Don't laugh. If you'd been there and seen someone walking on the water in the moonlight, what would you have thought?)

Jesus calmed their fears and told them not to be afraid.

Then Peter called out, "Lord, if it's you . . . tell me to come to you on the water" (v. 28).

Jesus said, "Come" (v. 29). (Sometimes I wonder if at that moment Peter wished he could take back his request.)

Then Peter did something amazing. He got out of the boat and started walking on the water toward Jesus. Can you imagine how he and the other disciples felt at that moment? Peter was doing what they all knew was impossible.

Now, it's true that as soon as Peter looked around and saw the wind and waves, his faith weakened and he began to sink. But that's not the part of the story I want you to focus on. I want you to think about this: Peter never would have walked on the water if he hadn't stepped out of the boat.

> The simple fact is that you will never see your dream realized until you get up and do something about it.

Many people have a dream, and they even set goals and pray for God's guidance and provision. But they never put their plans into action. The simple fact is that you will never see your dream realized until you get up and do something about it. God never blesses good intentions. He blesses action. If you want to do great things for God, you need to cultivate the action habit.

Just Get Started

People often tell me they just can't get started. Sometimes this is due to fears (real or imagined). We have listened to our own inner critics too long, or someone close to us has said something that intimidated us.

I've learned a secret in my life that many others have discovered. The moment you start on your dream, the fear related to the dream immediately goes away. If you're scared, it's okay to feel the fear and take the first step anyway. As Woody Allen once said, "Eighty percent of success is just showing up."[1] Just show up and get started.

Do you want to get your degree? Pay a visit to the local community college admissions office and sign up for classes. Does your dream involve working for a certain company? Get dressed up and apply for a job there. Once you walk in, the fear usually goes away. And if it doesn't? Push through the fear and do it anyway.

Sometimes you may need to find creative solutions to your fear problem. I once heard of a salesman who was too intimidated to visit potential clients. He finally developed a creative solution to his dilemma. He would force himself to walk into a prospective client's office and say, "I'm here to meet Mr. so-and-so. Do you have a restroom I could use?" Then he would go into the restroom, get his bearings by looking in the mirror and talking to himself, and come out and meet the client. Just forcing himself to walk into the office helped him get past his fear.

Maybe you want to be a public speaker, and you even have a great presentation prepared, but you're afraid of rejection. If so, it's time to force yourself into doing a presentation for someone within the next week. If you can't make it happen that soon, try booking a talk for a group at your church, the local YMCA, the Boy Scouts, or even your child's school. The point is that once the date is set, you have to follow through. And when you walk on that stage, you kill the intimidation. Even if your presentation is a little rough, you'll learn something every speaker has discovered: "I didn't die."

Pride is another hurdle that can keep us from getting started. Sometimes we have to get past our egos and accept the fact that when we start something new, we will probably look bad at first. If you want to get in great shape, you need to join a gym while you're still out of shape. Have you ever avoided the gym because you didn't want to be embarrassed? Or maybe you didn't go to church because you thought you weren't spiritual enough? How do you think you get spiritual?

Sometimes you just have to give yourself permission to do something badly so you can finally get started. Suppose you're taking a class in sculpture. When you're a beginner, you might start with an ugly lump of clay and finish with an ugly lump of clay. But if you stick with it, your skills will improve.

I have a confession to make. I'm not a good writer. If you don't believe me, just ask my publisher. I have found that my goal is no longer to write well. My goal is just to write. If I keep at it, I will eventually have something that can be shaped and edited into something good.

Writers write. Singers sing. Actors act. Just keep developing your craft and people will eventually come alongside you to help you improve. I now have a team of people who help me by editing my writing so that by the time you read it, it's actually good.

If you're at the gym and can't figure out how to start getting in shape, ask someone to show you what to do. If you are trying to start a business, take a local businessperson to lunch and ask them a ton of questions. People love to help others succeed. Others will help you if you ask them.

Some years ago, Nike had a slogan: "Just do it!" That's how you get started. You just do it.

Maintain Your Momentum

It's official. You are on your way to fulfilling your God-given dreams. You sold your first item. You are now a church attender. You are now a public speaker. You are no longer intimidated, or, at the very least, you are less intimidated than before. Every day moves you one step closer to your goal. So how do you keep up the momentum?

Do Something Every Day

Many people think about what they want to do but never do anything about it. Some start out strong but fizzle out. People who have developed the action habit do something every day to help their dreams become a reality. Even if they are moving slowly, they are moving forward—daily.

What are you going to do *today* that moves you closer to accomplishing your goals?

Recently, I read a book by Robert Allen, a real estate investor and author, and he said something that applies to the action habit. He was speaking of real estate, but the point is still valuable for you regardless of your dreams. "Don't wait to buy real estate. Buy real estate and wait."[2] In other words, if you are not astute at finding good deals in real estate, just buy an okay deal, rent it out, hold on to it, and over time that okay price will still make you money. The point is to get started working on your dream today.

God is a God of now. God does not want us to focus on tomorrow at the expense of today. The Bible says, "Now faith is being sure of what we hope for, being convinced of what we do not see" (Heb. 11:1 NET). Delayed faith is really just fear. Real faith is now faith. If this book just increases your knowledge but doesn't move you to action, then you have wasted your time and money. God wants to make your faith come alive.

It's time to get to work. Start doing something today and every day to work toward your dream. Life is too short to put off living any longer.

Stop Making Excuses

Many people never get started working on their dreams because they're always making excuses. There's always something more important to do. Or they ran out of time today but will get to it tomorrow. Or they don't have the resources or money they need to get started. If you want to start moving toward your dream, you need to recognize excuses for what they are: dream killers.

I have a friend named Judah. Judah is a leader. He is always on the move, getting things done. He is the president of a nonprofit organization that hosts an annual concert as well as several small concerts and events every year to promote the cause of Christ. Thousands of people gather at these events, and many have been touched by this young man's influence. The amazing part is that Judah cannot walk. He is a quadriplegic and completely confined to a wheelchair. But he has not allowed his limitations to keep him from making an impact and reaching for his dreams.

> Someone in the world is facing the same situation you are but is reaching their dream.

Are you making excuses? You may think you have a good excuse, but I promise you that someone in the world is facing the same situation you are but is reaching their dream. Bishop T. D. Jakes once said, "Someone who has been given a worse hand in life than you is winning with it."[3] Ouch! It hurts, but you know it's true.

Become a Doer

I have had the privilege of meeting many people over the years. When I travel and speak at events, conferences, and churches, I'm often introduced to people of influence. These are the movers and shakers, the big givers for the event, the people behind the scenes who are organizing everything, and so on. Whenever I meet leaders who are major players in their communities, people of influence and means, I notice that these leaders are very different from one another.

Some are well educated. Some aren't. Some are good looking; others have great personalities. Some are very personable and outgoing; others are shy. In other words, there is no success-type personality. The only common characteristic I've found among all these successful people is this: they are doers. When you are a doer, you are action oriented, always moving forward. Walt Disney once said, "We don't look backwards for very long. We keep moving forward, opening up new doors and doing new things . . . and curiosity keeps leading us down new paths."[4]

The New Testament tells Christians to "be doers of the word, and not hearers only" (James 1:22 ESV). God wants you to be a person of action. You may not be where you want to be, but if you keep moving forward, you will know in your heart you are on your way.

Break Down Your Goals

If your goals are large and you feel overwhelmed, break them down into bite-sized chunks. You've probably heard the joke, "How do you eat an elephant? One bite at a time." It may be silly, but the principle is sound. Gigantic goals can overwhelm you, but if you reduce them to smaller, more reachable goals, you'll be surprised how much less stressed you feel.

How do you break down your goals into bite-sized chunks? There are many approaches, but one of the easiest is to ask, "What is the next thing I have to do if I want to reach this goal?" Once you've identified the next step in reaching your larger goal, complete it. Then go on to the next step.

For example, suppose your goal requires your income taxes be completed early, to be able to get a bank loan toward a major purchase tied to your goals. If you feel overwhelmed, don't focus on the big picture. Instead, think about one thing you need to do to finish that task. One step could be gathering your W-2s and other documents. Next, you could gather receipts for medical expenses or other deductions, and so on.

By breaking down your goals into smaller and more manageable steps, you'll find it much easier to get into the action habit.

Keep Your Goals in Front of You

If you want to get into the action habit, you need to carry your goals with you at all times. People tease me because I still carry around a paper day-planning notebook, but it works for me. Whether they're on your iPhone, Blackberry, laptop, iPad, Kindle, paper planner, or even a 3 x 5 index card, keep your goals with you. Each morning or evening, make a list of what you need to do that day (or the next morning) to move one step closer to your goals.

My most productive moments happen when I have a to-do list in front of me. I love the endorphin rush I feel when I check off something. Have you ever finished a task that wasn't on your list but you added it to the list just so you could check it off? People who are in the action habit will not be denied the "high" of accomplishment.

God Created You for a Purpose

You will feel most alive when you are working toward your goals because God created you to find purpose in those tasks. You are most connected to your Creator when you are doing what he made you to do.

Worship is connecting to God, but this does not just happen when we go to church and sing to him. Worship happens when we do our best for him. The apostle Paul wrote to one church, "Whatever you do, work at it with all your heart, as working for the Lord, not for human masters" (Col. 3:23). When you pour yourself into your God-given dreams, you will experience a sense of accomplishment far superior to what you feel when you simply think about them.

My father worked for NASA during the glory years in Houston. He was a draftsman during the Apollo missions, and some of his closest friends are still in the space program. He once told me that a lot of fuel is required to get into space. In fact, you need a swimming pool of fuel per second just to break free of the earth's gravity and get into space. Yet once the space shuttle reached orbit, it could run on the same amount of fuel as a large SUV.

> **You are most connected to your Creator when you are doing what he made you to do.**

Getting started on a dream may require more fuel than you can imagine. You may have to burn a ton of time, money, and energy to get started, but once you are in "orbit"—in the realm of your dream—the effort required to stay there will be less. But as you expend those initial efforts, remember that where you are heading few will ever go.

One of the best ways to get into the action habit is to take one of your larger goals and break it down into manageable tasks or subgoals. For this exercise, get your notebook and a pen or pencil and find a quiet place where you won't be disturbed.

1. In your notebook, list two or three of your largest and most intimidating goals.

2. Choose one of those three (preferably the most important goal), and then ask yourself, "What is the very first thing I have to do to move toward this goal?" Write it down in your notebook with the number 1 by it.

3. Ask yourself what comes next. Write that down with the number 2 beside it. Continue listing the steps toward your goal until you've written down all the necessary steps.

4. Once you've completed your list, go back and turn number 1 into an action item. Continue to make each step into an action item, complete with deadline dates.

Now that you have the idea, just do it!

8

STRENGTHEN
Your Confidence

• • • • •

In chapter 7, we learned about developing the action habit. Unfortunately, many people never take the steps necessary to reach their dreams. Often they lack confidence. A lack of confidence is a close cousin of fear, and it is equally powerful in preventing us from pursuing our dreams. If you have ever found yourself in need of confidence to take that next step in life, this chapter is for you.

I have spent years studying confident people, and I have also found that the Bible has a lot to say about confidence. Unfortunately, most of the writing on this topic is found in psychology and positive-thinking books, and they tend to set off warning buzzers in the minds of Christians. As you read this chapter, remember that all truth originates with God. What I have found may have been confirmed by the world's leading psychologists, but the Bible said it long before those psychologists were born.

So how do you develop confidence, particularly when you are facing a daunting challenge? Is it possible to transform how you think? Not only is it possible, but if you follow these steps, it is actually predictable. But first you have to open your mind to a new way of thinking.

A remarkable verse in the book of Romans tells us, "Don't copy the behavior and customs of this world, but let God transform you into a new person by changing the way you think" (12:2 NLT). At first glance, you may think this verse means that once you are a Christian, you no longer think evil thoughts but instead think good thoughts. Although that is true, I believe there is more to it than this.

For example, suppose you were once a guy without Christ who went to bars and thought only about sleeping with women, partying, getting more money for yourself, and so on. Then you became a Christian, and now you are living for Christ, trying to honor him and live a pure life. At face value, this Scripture passage means, "Think evil thoughts and you'll live an evil, self-ish life. Think good thoughts and you'll live a good, healthy life."

That's right. But the meaning of the verse goes deeper than just ridding your mind of selfish desires. The idea is that you should be transformed by filling your mind with the fullness of Christ and thinking at the highest level of your potential in him. Another way to say it is, "Think amazingly huge thoughts and you can live an amazingly huge life."

In my experience, living life at a higher level does not require skills and abilities at that level. It requires thinking at that level and increasing your capacity to live there. If you can take control of how you think, you can take greater control of your life. If you want to live like someone else, don't just emulate what they do; learn to think like they think.

I can imagine what you're thinking right about now. "Okay, Cornelius, that's easy for you to say. But how am I supposed to learn how to think differently? How can I build that confidence?"

I'm glad you asked.

Borrow Confidence from Others

Yes, you read that heading correctly. You can actually "borrow" confidence until you develop your own. How do you do that? By finding a mentor.

People tend to be confident in what they have already done. For example, I do not have to psych myself up to drive a car, because I do it every day. No extra confidence needed, because I already have it. But my son, who is entering driver's education this year, is nervous when he gets behind the wheel. Why? Because he's never driven a car—yet. When he takes driver's education, he will operate a car with an experienced driver—a driving mentor—in the seat beside him. He'll still be nervous, but the presence and guidance of his driving mentor will give him confidence he didn't have before.

The power of a mentor is that they have already done something you want to learn to do. You will not just gain their knowledge when you are around them. You will also gain their confidence.

When I spend time with my pastor-mentors, I realize that what I find intimidating they have already done. What's more, they talk about those things as if they are no big deal. Because they've already done them, those things are no longer frightening. I gain confidence from my mentors because I know that I'm getting the inside track on how to do certain things. I'm learning from people who have already done what I want to do. Being exposed to that level of expertise is invaluable to me.

Years ago, I prayed this prayer: "God, I don't have to be rich, but please make me rich in relationships." Over the years, God has answered that prayer repeatedly. Here are a few lessons I've learned about developing great mentoring relationships.

Start with Books and Recordings

One of the easiest (and least expensive) steps to learning anything is through books and audio or video recordings. No matter what the area in which you need to develop confidence, I can pretty much guarantee there's at least one book, podcast, lecture series, website, or online seminar about it. And chances are, there are more resources out there than you'll have the time to explore.

> **Just by reading, you can meet with the most amazing people and gain access to their best thoughts anytime you want.**

For example, one of your dreams may be to become an outstanding parent, but right now you are looking at your newborn baby in fear. A few good parenting books can ease your fears with every chapter you read.

Someone once told me that books are people. In other words, when you read a book, you are getting the sum of the best thoughts, experiences, and ideas from the author. Just by reading, you can meet with the most amazing people and gain access to their best thoughts anytime you want. The same holds true with audio and video resources, podcasts, websites, and so on.

If you're on a budget and you want to grow your confidence, this is the place to start.

Attend Seminars and Conferences

Books and recordings are great, but they have one major weakness. You can't interact with them. If consulting resources is all you do, you'll eventually hit a plateau and stop growing. Your next step in finding a mentor needs to be interpersonal.

For example, a beginning writer can learn a lot from books, magazines, and tapes about writing and publishing. But most writers will tell you that eventually you need to join a critique group so you can get honest feedback on your writing. This holds true with any area in which you hope to grow and gain confidence. Sooner or later you need the input of others.

You may find this input by attending seminars and workshops. After the sessions, you'll have the chance to talk with others who are farther along on the journey than you. You may also have the opportunity to ask specific questions of the teachers or workshop leaders. Seminars and workshops can also give you the opportunity to grow and gain confidence by actually doing what you're afraid of. Many people who need to learn how to speak in public have been helped by joining Toastmasters or taking the Dale Carnegie course. Depending on what you're trying to learn, a local community college may be a resource.

> **Find ways to meet people who are doing what you want to do, and learn from their experience.**

Bottom line? Don't try to learn in a vacuum (totally on your own). Find ways to meet people who are doing what you want to do, and learn from their experience.

Find a Personal Mentor or Coach

If you really want to excel, you'll ultimately need more than books and seminars. You'll need to find a personal mentor. This is the most extensive level of confidence building yet often the most overlooked.

A personal (one-on-one) mentor works with you directly. It can be a short-term situation in which you sit down with an expert and pick his or her brain. For example, maybe you want to grow in your faith and have already read a bunch of books and attended a few weekend retreats and Bible conferences. This is where you offer to take your pastor to dinner, ask questions, and find out what he would do if he were in your shoes.

A mentoring relationship can also be long-term. Perhaps someone in your church or community has skills you wish to learn. If you have a teachable attitude and a genuine desire to learn, you may be surprised at how easy it is to find someone to be your personal mentor. Having a mentor may cost you some money—and it will certainly cost you time—but the rewards will be tangible. You gain confidence and skills you otherwise wouldn't have had.

If you're thinking mentoring could get expensive, you're correct. However, I don't look at this as an expense; I regard it as an investment. I've found that the best personal investment I can make is in my own learning.

If you are looking to borrow confidence, you can't cut the process short. If you want to become an expert—or even competent—in a particular field, you need to follow certain steps. If you try to skip over some steps and go straight to the top, you will almost certainly fall down and find yourself starting over at step one. As Zig Ziglar used to say, "The elevator to success is broken, so everyone has to take the stairs."[1]

Borrow Confidence from Your Future

Another way to build confidence is by borrowing it from your future. Athletes practice this regularly. They're taught to create a mental picture of themselves hitting a home run, making the winning shot, or completing the perfect dive. This confidence builder is called visualization, and though it has been extensively researched in the self-development field, you can also find it in the Bible.

Consider King David. What would make David go from tending sheep in a field to being an assistant to a king to taking on an undefeated fighting champion? The answer could be that David knew in his heart he was the next king. The prophet Samuel had come to his house and anointed him—a boy—to be the next king of Israel. David knew God had chosen him, and he believed in who he would be in the future, not just who he was in the present.

When David faced Goliath, he knew the victory was already his. He knew he would win. He looked up at Goliath and said, "This is the LORD's battle, and he will give you to us" (1 Sam. 17:47 NLT).

I wonder how many times David visualized himself as king while he was alone watching sheep in his father's pasture.

Psychologists tell us that our emotions don't recognize the difference between what is real and what is imaginary. This explains why a man's wife might wake up mad at him after she dreams he cheated on her.

If you don't believe this to be a fact, try this exercise and see for yourself. Imagine you're taking a bite out of a slice of chocolate cake (if you don't like chocolate cake, think of some food you do like). Don't just think about it. Close your eyes and see the cake in your mind, all seven glorious layers. See the thick frosting between each layer and the chunks of dark chocolate on top. Now imagine that your fork is cutting through the cake, and as you put a piece of that luscious chocolate on your tongue, it melts and floods your mouth with rich flavor. Did your mouth water? I bet it did.

All you did was picture the cake in your mind, yet you experienced the feelings and the physiological phenomena that come with actually eating chocolate cake—without the calories, of course.

You can use the same technique to build your confidence. By visualizing yourself doing something and succeeding, you can develop the confidence you need to accomplish the things God has laid on your heart.

Change Your Self-Talk

Similar to visualization is self-talk. Self-talk is what we tell ourselves about ourselves. Unfortunately, most of that talk is negative. According to behavioral psychologist and author Dr. Shad Helmstetter, by the time the average person turns eighteen, he has been told no or what he can't do about 148,000 times.[2] Let's assume your parents were outstanding and encouraging souls. In that case, you were told about your limits and what you couldn't do only 100,000 times by the time you became an adult. This doesn't mean your parents were evil. In their efforts to protect you and keep you from being hurt, they told you no repeatedly.

Here's the problem with this. Repetition is a convincing argument. If we are told (or tell ourselves) something often enough, we believe it. And unfortunately, most of us are much better at telling ourselves what we can't do than affirming what we can do. In fact, behavioral researchers tell us that 77 percent of what we think or say to ourselves is negative, counterproductive, and works against us.[3] It's time to change that. The good thing about self-talk is it can work both ways. Although negative self-talk is damaging, positive self-talk is empowering.

In my book *I Dare You to Change*, I tell the story of Gideon from Judges 6. When God appeared to Gideon, he addressed him as a "mighty warrior" (Judg. 6:12). But at that moment, Gideon was cowering in a winepress (generally a low-lying area) and hiding from Israel's enemies, the Midianites. Gideon was frozen, fearing for his life. But God infused confidence into him, not by addressing him as he was but by describing what he would become—a mighty and courageous warrior. Gideon needed to hear what God thought of him because he did not believe in himself.[4]

One word from God can change how you feel about yourself. If you are doubtful of your ability, you may want to read what God has to say about you. Just a quick look through the Bible shows that God thinks a lot of you.

- "The Lord will make you the head, not the tail. If you pay attention to the commands of the Lord your God that I give you this day and carefully follow them, you will always be at the top, never at the bottom" (Deut. 28:13).

- "But you are a chosen race, a royal priesthood, a holy nation, a people for God's own possession, so that you may proclaim the excellencies of Him who has called you out of darkness into His marvelous light" (1 Pet. 2:9 NASB).

- "For I can do everything through Christ, who gives me strength" (Phil. 4:13 NLT).

- "No, in all these things we are more than conquerors through him who loved us" (Rom. 8:37).

- "If God is for us, who can be against us?" (Rom. 8:31).

If this is what God says about us, why are we so negative toward ourselves?

Now, here's some good news. Just as a computer can run only the software program recorded on its hard drive—and that programming can be changed—you can erase your old negative programming and replace it with positive programming. You can learn to replace your negative thoughts that are limiting you with a new program.

The Bible actually gives us some insight into David's ability to change his mental state. On one occasion, before he was king, David came home with his men from battle to find that enemies had attacked and taken all their possessions and, even worse, their families. David's men were so furious that they thought about killing him.

David was in complete despair and fearful for his family as well as his own life. David then did something that gives us great insight into how to change our mental state: "David was greatly distressed . . . but David encouraged himself in the LORD his God" (1 Sam. 30:6 KJV).

After David talked to himself and affirmed that he could do something about his situation, he rallied himself and his men, and they routed the enemy, rescued their families, and recovered their property. Just as David did, it's time we rewrite our mental programming and begin to affirm our value, our possibilities, and our abilities.

What I'm going to ask you to do next is legitimate both biblically and psychologically. I'm going to ask you to follow the prescription for affirming yourself found in the book of Joel: "Let the weak say, I am strong" (3:10 KJV). Based on this Scripture passage, I want you to write out an affirmation. First, choose one of your dreams that, deep down, you don't believe you can accomplish. Then write out an affirmation that fits the style and tense of Joel 3:10. Here are some steps to follow.

Write It in the Affirmative

Make sure you write out your affirmation as a positive statement. For example, you wouldn't write, "I'm no longer broke," but rather, "I am wealthy." Or maybe you are having a hard time believing you can lose weight and be healthy. You would not write, "I'm no longer fat." You would instead write, "I am healthy, I eat right, and I look and feel great."

Write It in the Present Tense

Another point to remember is that the verse does not say, "Let the weak say I am going to be strong." It says, "Let the weak say I *am* strong." So your affirmation for dealing with guilt and shame would look something like this: "I am forgiven. I am pure. I am new in Christ."

Say It Aloud

Note that the verse does not say, "Let the weak think I am strong." It says, "Let the weak *say* I am strong." Once you have an affirmation written that fits what you are trying to change, say it out loud to yourself.

Repeat the Affirmation

Repetition is the key to building confidence. If you heard someone say, "You're ugly" one time, it probably would bother you for a moment, but in time you'd forget it. Yet if someone said that to you repeatedly every day of your entire life, not only would you believe it, but it would also be very difficult to convince you otherwise. If you've been told over and over by others or by your own inner critic that you "can't do this," "can't have that," "don't deserve this," you must stand up to the negative programming and say, "Enough!"

This is why God tells us to meditate on Scripture day and night. "Keep this Book of the Law always on your lips; meditate on it day and night, so that you may be careful to do everything written in it. Then you will be prosperous and successful" (Josh. 1:8).

Don't wait. Begin reprogramming your mind now so that when the next opportunity comes your way you will not have to battle the negative thoughts standing in the way of your future. The reason this is so important is that, over time, we become what we most believe about ourselves. You can change what you believe about yourself by changing what you say. There is a miracle in your mouth.

> **Begin reprogramming your mind now so that when the next opportunity comes your way you will not have to battle the negative thoughts standing in the way of your future.**

Once you begin to speak this new reality into your life, begin to act accordingly. For example, if you say, "I am in love with my spouse," then you must act as if you're in love. You might respond, "But I don't feel in love." It doesn't matter. Act your way into feeling in love. If you consistently act as if you're in love, your actions will change not only how you see your spouse but also how they see you.

David believed he would be king. He also believed he could kill Goliath. David visualized success, spoke it aloud, and acted it out in real life. This should be reason enough for you to begin visualizing your success, affirming yourself verbally, and living out your dreams.

If this is not reason enough, I'd like to leave you with one more motivating thought. Once you achieve your dream, what initially seems to you a great accomplishment will eventually become your new normal. More important, it will impact those around you.

David killed Goliath. That was awesome in and of itself. But because David was a giant killer, his sons became giant killers also (see 2 Sam. 21:15–22).

What you overcome will be normal to your kids. If you overcome selfishness by learning to tithe, your kids will tithe without struggle. Why? Because it will be normal to them. If you overcome pride, your kids will be humble. Why? Because they saw you humble yourself. What you do, your kids will do.

My father taught me how to buy a house and keep our first house as a rental property, and I am forever grateful. A few years later, my wife and I decided to buy a small apartment complex. We were terrified but just told ourselves repeatedly, "This will work." Now my kids are going to think it's normal for everyone to own their own apartment complex. What are my grandkids going to think is normal?

Build your confidence. Your future is worth it. The next generation is waiting for you to show the way.

Psychologists tell us it takes twenty-one days to form a new habit. The reason it takes this long is that you are cutting a new neurological trail in your mind that automatically makes you think and act a certain way. I challenge you to work through the steps given above and create an affirmation related to your dream. Then for the next twenty-one days, wake up every day and read your affirmation to yourself as you look in the mirror. Repeat this once in the afternoon and once at night.

9

BUILD MOMENTUM
through Diligence

• • • • •

A young man named Todd Helton wanted to excel at baseball, and he asked his father to help him. So his father built a batting cage in their backyard out of chicken wire and fence posts and then bought a used pitching machine. He then told his son that if he wanted to become really good at baseball, he should practice hitting the ball every day.

"How long should I practice?" Todd asked.

"Swing until your hands bleed," his dad replied.

Todd took his father's advice, and now he plays for the Colorado Rockies. He is also considered one of the greatest batters of his generation.

Does the advice Todd's father gave him sound a bit over-the-top to you? If it does, try doing a Google search on "Olympic training routines." Athletes who want to achieve at the Olympic or professional level devote hours to practicing and training.

Right now you may be thinking, *But I don't want to be an Olympic athlete or any other kind of athlete.* It doesn't matter.

The same principle applies to musicians, performers, and writers who want to reach the top of their craft. It also applies to you. The bottom line is that there is no such thing as achievement without hard work.

You've decided to take action on your dream. You're building confidence. But how do you take things to the next level? How do you gain the momentum that will enable you to excel?

Call it focus; call it persistence; call it hard work; call it perseverance; call it whatever you want. I call it diligence. You build and maintain momentum through diligence. If you want to excel and be truly successful, there is no other path to follow.

> **You build and maintain momentum through diligence.**

We live in a time when people want quick and easy success. Newbie writers expect their first book to make the *New York Times* bestseller list. Fledgling musicians and entertainers hope for instant celebrity through reality programs such as *American Idol*. And people all across the country buy lottery tickets with money they can't afford to spend because they're hoping for a shortcut to wealth. And while it's true that some people are overnight successes, they are the exception, not the rule. For the other 99 percent of us, diligence is the pathway to achievement.

So what does diligence look like? Diligence is reflected in the things you do, the choices you make, and the habits you develop.

A Diligent Person Works Hard

Scripture teaches us that idleness is not good. The book of Proverbs says, "Work hard and become a leader; be lazy and become a slave" (12:24 NLT). One harsh truth that you must come to terms with is this: no one is going to accomplish your dreams for you.

When I was pastoring with no staff and no friends in a little church in Corpus Christi, I had a revelation that if I was going to succeed, it was going to be up to me. No one was coming to bail me out or hand me success on a platter. This motivated me to get moving. I am very aware that without the Lord we would not have succeeded. However, I've known plenty of godly church planters who failed because they did not work hard. If you want to realize your dreams, you must put in the effort yourself.

Malcolm Gladwell, author of the book *Outliers: The Story of Success*, suggests that it takes ten thousand hours to achieve success in any field.[1] You must be willing to put in long hours before you can expect to see the outcomes you are looking for. The results will eventually come, but they take time and effort.

A Diligent Person Does the Hard Things First

Let's face it, we all have unpleasant tasks to complete in the pursuit of our dreams. Brian Tracy compares doing these difficult, unpleasant tasks to eating live frogs. In his bestselling book, *Eat That Frog*, Tracy says, "If you have to eat a live frog . . . it doesn't pay to sit and look at it very long."[2] The principle is simple and direct. If you have a list of things to do, do the hardest one first and the rest of the day will seem easy.

Maybe you have a big task that you're avoiding. That one task, if ignored, will completely shut down your progress and could keep you from reaching your goals. Don't allow a difficult task to hold you back.

A Diligent Person Doesn't Make Excuses

Many people suffer from a malady called excusitis. Those who have excusitis tend to talk big about the things they are going to do, but when they fail to produce results, they have an excuse ready. Generally, those excuses involve pointing the finger of responsibility everywhere but at themselves. Their failure is someone else's fault. Or the circumstances weren't right. Or they ran out of time. Or they were sick. Or they're still in the planning stage. Or they're still praying about what to do. Their favorite phrase seems to be, "I'd have achieved my dream, but . . ."

If you are still praying about getting started on a dream, my question for you is direct: How long are you going to pray? Don't get me wrong. Prayer isn't just important; it's essential. But there comes a time when you have to get moving.

When Moses saw Pharaoh's army pursuing him and trapping the newly born nation of Israel up against the Red Sea, he boldly told the people to stand still and watch God rescue them (Exod. 14:13–14). But in the next verse, God says to Moses, "Why are you crying out to me? Tell the people to get moving" (Exod. 14:15 NLT). Evidently, after making his bold proclamation, Moses prayed a "God, what are we going to do now?" type of prayer. God told him to stop praying and get moving—and then God parted the Red Sea so they could walk across to freedom.

Sooner or later you have to start moving. If your excuse is, "I'm still planning," let me ask you this. How long are you planning on planning? You can plan your dream to death. When are you going to do something? Jesus died so you can live a full life through him. He gave you his Word, his power through the Holy Spirit, and a dream. Stop planning and start working toward your dream.

Your reputation is on the line. Either you are going to continue to talk big, or you are going to start living big. Henry Ford once said, "You can't build a reputation on what you're going to do."[3]

A Diligent Person Strives for Excellence

Achieving a big dream is like running a marathon. Unfortunately, most people approach it as if it were a sprint. They begin with a burst of energy and enthusiasm, but as time passes—and fatigue sets in—they become weary and quit.

Distance runners train so they can run farther. If they didn't train, they would run out of energy long before completing the 26.2 miles in a marathon. Training is dull, boring, and tedious work, but athletes who want to reach the pinnacle of success strive for excellence. Training changes how far and how fast they can go. They increase their speed and distance by doing a little more, going a little faster every day.

Athletes need skill, but without diligence, skill is wasted. What sets you apart in life is not your talent, your education, your connections, or your intellect. What will make you stand out is your ability to keep going when others quit. If you cultivate diligence and develop your skill, you may be surprised how far they take you. The book of Proverbs has some encouraging words for the diligent: "Do you see a man who excels in his work? He will stand before kings; he will not stand before unknown men" (22:29 NKJV).

You may be thinking, *I just clean houses* or *I only hang drywall.* Maybe so, but if you're diligent in your work and strive for excellence in what you do, you could ultimately find yourself standing before "kings." You may end up hanging drywall in the governor's mansion. The point of the proverb is that if you strive for excellence, you will rise to the top in whatever you're doing.

I have a friend who used to play pro football. His name is Aeneas Williams. I said to Aeneas once over dinner, "You know, Aeneas, I could be a pro player too."

He looked at me skeptically and said, "Is that so?"

I said, "Yeah. I just need everyone else to slow down."

I won't ever play in the NFL; I don't have the physical ability. However, by getting to know a pro athlete like Aeneas Williams, I have learned what it takes to be excellent in any endeavor. Pro athletes do not excel because of what they do on the field but because of what they do off the field, in practice. They develop their excellence in the weight room and on the practice field when no one is there to cheer them on.

Your dream may not be to become a pro athlete, but when it comes to striving for excellence, here are three things I've learned from them.

First, pro athletes hone their skills to perfection. (This applies to professionals in any area.) They do everything with excellence and with a level of quality that few can match. If you wish to excel, you must raise the bar on the quality of what you do. Don't settle for mediocre work. Do your very best all the time—and then keep raising the bar. Always be improving.

> If you wish to excel, you must be prepared to keep training, growing, and learning.

Second, pros never stop training. Even for a gifted athlete, success comes only with endless amounts of repetition. If you wish to excel, you must be prepared to keep training, growing, and learning.

Third, pros play through pain. True professionals do not leave the game with every ache and pain. They're committed to reaching the team's goal, and if that means shaking off pain and continuing to play, so be it. If you want to excel, you must be committed to pursuing your dream whether you feel like it or not. You do not let someone throw you off your game because they hurt your feelings. You do not let setbacks stop you in your tracks. You do not give in to discouragement. You do not let naysayers convince you that your head is in the clouds.

A Diligent Person Develops Good Habits

It's one thing to read about the practices of a diligent person. It's another thing entirely to incorporate those practices into your daily life. If you want to be consistently successful, you must cultivate good habits. The problem is that most of us have already developed a bunch of bad habits. Diligence means we're always working to get rid of the bad habits and replace them with good ones. As you probably already know, this is not an easy process.

I wish discipline came naturally, but for most of us it doesn't. I'm sure you can relate to the apostle Paul as well as I can when he expressed his frustration over his inability to live the way he wanted to. He wrote in the book of Romans, "I don't really understand myself, for I want to do what is right, but I don't do it. Instead, I do what I hate. . . . So I am not the one doing wrong; it is sin living in me that does it" (7:15, 17 NLT).

Here are three steps we must take if we're to develop good habits and achieve our God-given dreams.

Stop (Eliminate Bad Habits and Time Wasters)[4]

We all have practices and habits that at best interfere with our progress and at worst are self-destructive. If you are serious about achieving your dreams, you will eliminate those things.

What holds you back and keeps you from reaching your dreams? Here are some things to consider.

If you lack the energy to pursue your God-given dreams, you may want to look at your health. If you are eating poorly, not exercising regularly, and staying up half the night, you will lack the physical and emotional vitality needed to push forward.

Maybe you feel you do not have time to work on your dreams. If so, you may want to determine how much time you spend in front of the television or on the internet. Spending time on social media may keep your "status" up-to-date, but how's the status on your goals? Scripture tells us that "the fruit of the Spirit is . . . self-control" (Gal. 5:22–23). As you examine your life, ask God to show you where you need to develop self-control.

Eliminating bad habits is important, but if you're committed to excellence, you also need to consider eliminating activities, practices, and hobbies that may be good but are still not helpful. They may be activities that drain your energy, use up your time, or change your focus.

Have you ever said something like, "I'd like to pursue my dream, but I've got too much on my plate?" If you have, you may need to think about getting a few of those things off your plate so you have time to work on what matters most. The apostle Paul told the Corinthian church, "You say, 'I am allowed to do anything'—but not everything is good for you. And even though 'I am allowed to do anything,' I must not become a slave to anything" (1 Cor. 6:12 NLT).

You now have a list of things to quit doing that have been holding you back. So what are you going to do with all this newfound free time on your hands? The book of Hebrews offers a suggestion: "Therefore, since we are surrounded by such a great cloud of witnesses, let us throw off everything that hinders and the sin that so easily entangles. And let us run with perseverance the race marked out for us" (12:1).

Start (Cultivate Productive Habits)

The second step we need to take if we're going to fulfill our purpose is to cultivate habits that increase our effectiveness. For example, maybe you need to start going to sleep earlier so you have more energy during your prime working hours. Or if one of your dreams is to have a thriving marriage, how about starting a regular date night with your spouse? One way to make sure you follow through is by lining up a standing babysitter. On that night, you pay the babysitter whether you go out or not. If your dream is to grow spiritually, it's time to start reading that daily devotion book that is sitting beside your bed.

As you consider the good habits you would like to cultivate, make sure they are aligned with your dreams. There's no reward for mere activity. Your activity needs to be moving you toward your goals. You may have a strong work ethic, but are you working on the right things? If you focus on the right action steps, you will see faster results than ever before. It's even possible to double your effectiveness without doubling your efforts.

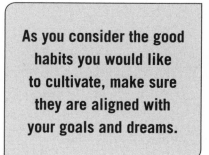

As you consider the good habits you would like to cultivate, make sure they are aligned with your goals and dreams.

How? Have you ever heard of the 80/20 principle? The 80/20 principle states that 80 percent of our results come from around 20 percent of our efforts. If you identify your top performing activities (the 20 percent), then you can eliminate time-wasting activities (the 80 percent) and replace them with your top producers.

For example, suppose you're a good writer but you haven't been progressing as quickly as you'd like. Writing is one of your top skills; it's part of the 20 percent. But to progress you need to make it a priority. You need to spend more time writing. So you look at your schedule and see that you're spending sixty minutes each day watching the news on TV. Why not stop watching the news (it's depressing anyway) and devote that time to your writing? You may be surprised at how much more you will accomplish.

Take the time to make a list of your top skills and activities and start investing more time doing those things. They will catapult you toward the realization of your dream.

You can do this. Paul told the Philippian church, "I can do all this through him who gives me strength" (Phil. 4:13). In this verse, the "can" comes before the "do" because this verse is intended to lead you into action. You cannot get a new result in your life until you start doing something different. Start today.

Continue (Build on Your Good Habits)

Finally, although there will be tasks to start and activities to stop, there will also be some things to continue. How do you know what those things are? If something you're doing is working, keep doing it. Then increase your efforts and do more of it.

In the early 1700s, Jacob Bernoulli, a noted Swiss mathematician, discovered what he called the law of large numbers. He said, "In any chance event, when the event happens repeatedly, the actual results will tend to be the calculated or planned results."[5] In other words, when you repeat actions toward an intended result over time, it almost becomes inevitable that you will get the result you are seeking. Of course, the Bible said this all along, as we saw earlier in Proverbs 22:29. The key is diligence.

While walking through an airport, I found myself drawn to a business book on display titled *The 10X Rule* by Grant Cardone. Cardone is an expert in sales and has built several multimillion-dollar companies. Although I do not agree with his personal beliefs, I do believe he has uncovered a principle found throughout the Bible.

"The *10X Rule* is based on understanding how much effort and thought are required to get anything done successfully. Chances are that if you look back over your life, you'll see that you have wildly underestimated both the actions and reasoning necessary to accomplish any endeavor to the point where it could be labeled successful."[6]

Cardone goes on to explain that the secret of success can be boiled down to simply applying more effort, specifically ten times the effort. "As I look back over my life, I see that the one thing that was most consistent with any success I've achieved was that I always put forth 10 times the amount of activity that others did."[7]

Let's say you have a teenager who wants to grow in the Lord. You want to help her gain spiritual momentum, but you're not sure how. She currently goes to church with you one hour a week. Over two months, that's eight hours of "God time." But suppose you send her to camp with the youth group, and she is there for five days. Assuming eight hours for sleep (which never happens), that's sixteen hours a day of God time for five days, or eighty hours. That's ten times the amount of time she normally focuses on God.

Scripture tells us, "A man reaps what he sows" (Gal. 6:7). It's time to step it up. If you sow more (ten times), you will reap more (ten times). If you build on your good habit, you will grow as a person and increase your ability to accomplish your God-given dreams.

• • •

How long and how hard should you work on your dreams? Remember the advice Todd Helton's father gave him. "Swing until your hands bleed." Every day go as long as you can and as hard as you can, and then go at it again the next day. If you are diligent, you will succeed.

For this exercise, make three lists in your notebook. Number them from 1 to 10 and title them "Stop," "Start," and "Continue."

Now take some time to think through the time wasters in your life. What are you doing and what habits do you have that are standing between you and your dreams? Write down as many as you can think of. After you've finished, do the same with things you need to start doing and things you need to continue doing.

Once you've written your lists, put a star by the two or three most important items on each list. Then write a specific action plan for each of them. For example, if on your stop list you wrote, "I watch too much TV," for your action plan, list a specific program you're going to stop watching. Next, go to your start or continue list and fill the extra time with one of those items. Let's say you decided to give up watching *Wheel of Fortune*. What are you going to do with those extra thirty minutes? Be specific.

Finally, once you've written your plan, stick to it!

10

Walk in

INTEGRITY

• • • • •

One day, a man and woman placed a carryout order at a fast-food chicken restaurant. The restaurant manager had just hidden that morning's cash receipts inside a to-go box, intending to deposit the money in the bank. Unfortunately, an employee accidentally gave the cash-filled box to the couple and did not realize her mistake until it was too late. The man and woman had already left with several thousand dollars.

As the manager and employee were panicking, the couple returned with the box and all the money. All they asked for was the chicken they had originally ordered.

The manager was blown away. "What integrity you both have," he told the couple. "Please stay here a moment while I get my camera. I want to take your picture and send it to the local newspaper."

The couple insisted that they wanted to remain anonymous. The manager persisted until the man said, "Look, I can't let you take that picture or even give you our names. You see, I'm married, and, well, this is not my wife."

Most of us, like that couple, are capable of demonstrating great integrity in one area yet make foolish choices in another. In today's world, the answer to the question of morals normally goes like this: "Do what feels good. Just don't get caught."

The problem with this line of reasoning is that it assumes that keeping a secret keeps you safe from any possible consequences. The reality is that when you lack integrity, you are being inconsistent with your actions and your beliefs. You may think you're living a God-honoring life, but the one area in which you are not honoring God affects everything else. To dishonor God is to cut off God's power from your life.

Not only that, but wrong choices set your life on a course heading toward disaster. Just ask a man who had an affair with his secretary or a woman who chose to flirt with her best friend's husband. They never thought they would be explaining to their children why Mommy and Daddy are no longer together.

Right choices can create the life you want. Wrong choices can bring disaster. The truth is that many people make right choices most of the time while simultaneously courting disaster. This is like taking two steps forward and one step back. One of the best ways to ensure you achieve your dreams is to stop taking steps backward.

Here are three steps that will help you strengthen your integrity.

Be Consistent

Another way to put this is, "Stop shooting yourself in the foot." If you eliminate the actions that are setting you back, you will consistently move forward. Although this sounds simple, it's not easy to accomplish.

Maybe you are hurting your chances for advancement at work because you do well on two projects only to blow a simple assignment after that. Because your boss can't trust you 100 percent, you don't advance. How great would it be if you quit setting yourself back with God and others by learning to be reliable and trustworthy? When your actions are consistent over the long haul, that consistency will breed trust and respect.

Building consistency into your life means you will move forward faster toward achieving your dreams. For example, you may eat right but not work out. As a result, your sedentary lifestyle choice offsets the benefits you should be enjoying from eating healthy. Or maybe you eat right and work out regularly, but you are not getting enough sleep. The stress caused by a lack of sleep can neutralize the benefits of exercise and proper eating.

Maybe you enjoy spending time with God in his Word, but you also fill your mind with television shows, movies, or music that are contrary to the Word of God and therefore neutralize the effectiveness of prayer and Bible study.

Here is an equation that reflects what many experience:

Two steps forward + one step back = barely any gains (after three moves, you're only one ahead)

Here is what you could be experiencing:

Two steps forward + a positive replacement step instead of the negative step = a multiplied return

One of the best ways to increase your success rate and avoid backward steps is to watch the environments you enter. For example, one of the ways I stay faithful in my marriage is by not going to bars or clubs. I even limit the hours I go to my gym. Some hours are what I call "family hours," and some are the "singles-hit-on-each-other hours." You know what I mean.

I also must be careful about TV and movies. I enjoy watching, but I have to limit my exposure to certain programs or channels. For you, this may not be an issue. In fact, you may need to avoid totally different things. Whatever you struggle with, make sure your actions do not place you in the path of temptation.

When your actions are consistent with your dreams, you eliminate backward steps and make steady progress forward.

Do What You Say You're Going to Do

Jesus said, "Let your Yes be simply Yes, and your No be simply No; anything more than that comes from the evil one" (Matt. 5:37 AMP). Simply put, follow through on your commitments. If you say you are going to help someone, help them. If you make a commitment, make sure you keep that commitment. Many of our greatest problems come because we fail to keep our promises. We go from promise makers to promise breakers rather than promise keepers.

Begin by resolving to keep your promises. The book of Psalms says that people of integrity "keep their promises, no matter what the cost" (15:4 CEV).

When you say you will be somewhere by 9 a.m., leave a few minutes early to make sure you arrive on time. How often do we show up late for an appointment and only offer a lame, "Sorry I'm late." That may work a few times, but sooner or later it will hurt you.

Instead of offering an excuse, what if you actually told the truth? "Hey, I was going to say, 'Sorry I'm late,' but you've heard that a lot. The truth is I've grown comfortable with making you wait because I think my time is more valuable than yours." Ouch. Not so nice to hear it that way.

The next time you're late, don't make excuses or lame apologies. Instead, apologize and promise to work on your tardiness. Then follow through by giving yourself more time or arranging your schedule so that you can arrive on time.

One of the biggest struggles I have is overcommitment. As I've studied the habits and practices of successful leaders, I've discovered that even though their ministries are much larger than mine, they do less than I do. This always amazes me because they seem to be getting more and better results. Why is that? They accomplish more because they know how to balance their lives and do what they need to do instead of agreeing to do everything.

Have you ever been sitting in a meeting you agreed to go to only to be dying inside and kicking yourself for agreeing to participate? This is a dead giveaway that you're overcommitted. You should only say yes because you want to attend; otherwise, just say no.

No is one of the most positive and powerful words you can ever say. Saying no does not mean you are rejecting someone or something; rather, it means you have a divine yes, a clear direction mandated to you from God. If anything or anyone does not fit that divine yes, you simply say no. For me, this means I say no to most meetings, no to most speaking and travel opportunities, and no to activities that do not match my family's priorities. Learning to say no will set you free from the tyranny of the busy. If you do not learn to say no, you will find yourself caught up in the thick of thin things.

When you make commitments to God, make sure you keep those commitments too. "Do for God what you said you'd do—he is, after all, your God" (Ps. 76:11 Message). If you look closely at the Old Testament (you choose the book—any will do), you'll notice that the story often centers around God's people failing to keep their commitment to worship him alone. As a result, God removes his hand of blessing and protection from them. Those stories are not simply a historical record; they are there to remind us that when we do not keep our promises to God, he cannot trust us with his blessings.

> **If you do not learn to say no, you will find yourself caught up in the thick of thin things.**

It's true that Jesus gave his life for our sins, and we experience eternity with him if we commit our lives to him. Nevertheless, we can seriously damage our lives on this side of eternity by not making our allegiance to God a priority. When we dishonor God by not keeping our promise to obey and worship him only, he will allow us to experience life without his blessing and protection.

Just as we allow our own children to experience consequences to serve as a warning, God will do the same with us. When my daughter was very little, I'd tell her, "Sophie, do not run out into the street." She often disobeyed—until she experienced the consequences of her actions. I told her, "If you go out in the street again, I will give you a spanking." That may sound harsh and old-school compared to the way you parent, but every child is different, and that's what worked for Sophie because she is a little stubborn (like her daddy).

To her, that spanking was painful; however, the pain on her behind was nothing compared to the pain of being hit by a car.

Thus, as a loving father, I allowed her to experience a little pain to save her from something far worse.

Has God allowed you to take a spanking lately? It could be a warning. In fact, this chapter may be a warning for you. I've had my share of warnings from God, and when I listen, I always benefit. When I have ignored God's warnings, I have always experienced a setback. Worse, I've been hurt far more than I ever thought possible.

Maybe you have been playing with fire in your life through lust or flirting with someone other than your spouse. Or perhaps your credit card debt is starting to get your attention, yet you are still overspending, ignoring the signs that are warning you to get it under control before you go off a financial cliff.

Warnings are not meant to hurt; they are meant to help. Heed the warnings from God, because once you leave "his yard" and enter the dangerous streets of the world, the pain can be severe and life altering.

> **When we dishonor God by not keeping our promise to obey and worship him only, he will allow us to experience life without his blessing and protection.**

Make a commitment to quit wavering with your words and actions. If you say you are committed to God and his ways, then go all the way. No more back and forth, one day committed to him, the next day ignoring him. One weekend you're in church, the next weekend you miss. One day you are parent of the year, and the next day—well, let's just say you're glad it wasn't recorded and posted on YouTube. Make a commitment today and work to keep it.

Call Yourself Out So Others Won't Have To

When you find yourself doing something that is contrary to your values and beliefs, share your mistake or problem with someone who loves you. This is extremely difficult but essential. James (the brother of Jesus) wrote, "Confess to one another therefore your faults (your slips, your false steps, your offenses, your sins) and pray [also] for one another, that you may be healed and restored. . . . The earnest (heartfelt, continued) prayer of a righteous man makes tremendous power available [dynamic in its working]" (James 5:16 AMP).

Have you ever been caught in a failure loop? This happens when you commit a sin, feel guilty, and confess it to God. You feel better once you confess, but you don't share your struggle with anyone else. Before you know it, you find yourself repeating the same self-defeating habit or sin. Then the guilt returns, and you confess to God—again. After a few days, the guilt evaporates, and you repeat the cycle. After a while, the guilt you feel gets worse, and the law of diminishing returns kicks in. This means you have to increase the bad behavior to get the same payoff.

The law of diminishing returns is reflected in how an alcoholic's problem grows worse. He drinks a few too many, then repents. Over time, he has to consume more liquor to get the same high. He knows his actions are wrong, and he feels bad because his habit is out of control. Now, not only is he addicted to alcohol, but he's also depressed. His depression causes him to—you guessed it—drink more. His drinking ruins his relationships and his career. When this happens, the only thing he has left is the alcohol. And so he is caught in a failure loop, a downward spiral. As his desperation increases, so does his need for a bigger payoff from alcohol, until it ultimately costs him everything, even his life. James describes the process this way: "Then, after desire has conceived, it gives birth to sin; and sin, when it is full-grown, gives birth to death" (James 1:15).

For you, your problem may be laziness, gossip, alcohol, gluttony, lust, pornography, anger that leads to rage, or any number of other self-destructive, sinful behaviors. Once a habit of sinfulness is fully developed, the only solution is for you to "bust yourself." In other words, bring your problem or sin into the open and become accountable to someone.

If you're stuck in a downward spiral, a failure loop, accountability is the game changer. It is often the difference between repeating the failure and breaking the cycle. This does not mean you share your struggle with one person and are forever healed. Twenty years of pastoral experience has taught me that the need for accountability never really goes away. As you gain control over a problem or habit, you may not need accountability as often, but you still need it. I highly recommend you find someone you trust to whom you can pour out your heart. The only way the seed of sin can thrive is if it's covered in the soil of secrecy and lies.

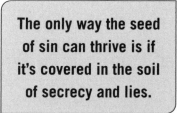

The only way the seed of sin can thrive is if it's covered in the soil of secrecy and lies.

What kind of person is a good candidate for an accountability partner? If you're married, your primary accountability partner should be your spouse. My wife knows the questions she needs to ask me regularly because she knows where I am weak. Don't be shocked when you share your struggle with your spouse and they are not surprised. Remember, they live with you and know you better than anyone. What you have to share with them may hurt them deeply, but it is better to share it and stop the madness than to continue to live a lie. Depending on the severity of the situation, you and your spouse may need to see a Christian counselor. Either way, you need to share your burdens, or you two will never be one as the Bible says you are to be.

The next person to open up to is a close friend. If you have never developed a deep, close friendship, doing so can be scary at first. Just remember to proceed cautiously, and make sure the person is trustworthy. You don't want your private struggles plastered all over Facebook. Your accountability partner should be someone who loves you and will be a point of strength rather than an enabler. That's why your drinking buddy should not be the person who helps you stop drinking. Your accountability partner should also be someone of the same sex, especially if you are married. Sharing pain creates a bond, and you only want that kind of bond with your spouse and a trusted friend.

If I were a betting man, and if I knew you were accountable to someone on a regular basis, I would bet on your success. But if you have never entered into a vulnerable discussion with someone you love and made yourself accountable in areas in which you are weak, I would have to bet against you.

No one is strong all the time. Everyone has a bad day. Everyone has a weakness or two (or three). Making yourself accountable to others is both frightening and risky. However, if you take the risk and open up to someone you love, doing so could save your life.

If you want to walk in integrity, you need to become a student of yourself. You must recognize your struggles and deal with them appropriately. If you're not sure, ask God to make them clear to you. David put it this way: "Search me, God, and know my heart; test me and know my anxious thoughts. See if there is any offensive way in me, and lead me in the way everlasting" (Ps. 139:23–24).

If you ask God to reveal to you where you are weak and where you are offending him, he will show you. When he shows you, repent and take decisive action to hold yourself accountable. Your integrity is worth it. Your dreams depend on it.

For this exercise, find a quiet place where you can be alone with God. Spend time asking him to show you what things may be hindering your progress. Are there any areas of sin you need to confess? Are you caught in a failure loop? Be honest with yourself and with God.

Next, write down in your notebook those areas in your life where you need help (accountability). Commit those areas to God in prayer and ask him to help you find someone to whom you can be accountable.

Finally, make a specific plan for approaching your friend/spouse to seek their help.

Remember, God lifts up the humble. Be willing to humble yourself, and he has promised to lift you up.

Part 3

MOVING
to the Next Level

11

Stay in Your
GIFT MIX

• • • • •

Are you overwhelmed right now? Is your schedule controlling you, or are you controlling your schedule? Do you feel tired most of the time? Are you running in too many directions and feeling stressed by too many demands on your time? The fact that you are tired and overwhelmed should convince you that something needs to change.

Living with exhaustion because of an overwhelming schedule not only makes you unhappy but also can irritate the people around you. Soon you may find that the very people you are trying to help are criticizing you. And that leads to more frustration.

People who are truly successful in life may not be good at many things, but they know what they are good at and do those things in a big way. This chapter will teach you how to set aside the things you are not good at so you can concentrate on what will help you achieve your God-given dream.

You are not an accident. God designed and gifted you for a specific purpose. Often, when people are not accomplishing their goals—or they're moving too slowly—it's because they are not staying in their gift mix. Your gift mix is the unique set of talents, skills, and abilities God has given you. When you are operating in your gift mix, you have confidence, you enjoy what you're doing, and, most importantly, you're good at it.

> **People who are truly successful in life may not be good at many things, but they know what they are good at and do those things in a big way.**

What happens when you try operating outside your gift mix? Let's take a look at a situation in which the early Christians found themselves: "But as the believers rapidly multiplied, there were rumblings of discontent. The Greek-speaking believers complained about the Hebrew-speaking believers, saying that their widows were being discriminated against in the daily distribution of food" (Acts 6:1 NLT).

The early church leaders had a problem. Their own success was wearing them out. The church had grown quickly, and they were having a hard time keeping up with the responsibilities of a growing ministry. People were falling through the cracks, and needs were not being met. In this case, the Greek-speaking believers felt that their widows were being neglected when food was handed out. So they did what people usually do. They started grumbling. (That never happens in your organization, does it?)

Maybe for you the issue isn't a growing ministry. Maybe it's a growing family or a busy schedule. Perhaps you are saying yes to one too many responsibilities, and you are gasping for breath. Maybe you are a stay-at-home mom, and your family and household expectations are wearing you down. Or perhaps you have such a mess on your hands at the office that when you walk in and see the piles of papers spilling over your inbox, you shut down emotionally. Maybe you've already tried working harder, but you still find yourself slipping farther behind. You feel as if you're trying to keep a dozen plates spinning on poles as you jump from emergency to emergency and from crisis to crisis. There is a better way.

How did Jesus's followers respond to the dilemma they faced? They called a meeting of all the believers and told them to appoint seven men who could oversee the distribution of food. That's a good solution, but what's really amazing is what the disciples said when they suggested this plan. They said, "We apostles should spend our time teaching the word of God, not running a food program" (Acts 6:2 NLT).

I can imagine what you're thinking: "Did the disciples blow off hungry widows?" The answer is a resounding no! The disciples realized they could keep ministering to the widows' needs themselves (which obviously was not working), or they could delegate. One way you know you are leading well in your area of influence (family, church, business, etc.) is that you are able to delegate responsibilities to others.

Do Less, Not More

If you want to achieve more, you have to do less. If you feel stressed, overwhelmed, and burned out, chances are you're doing too much. The people I know who are extremely good at what they do and who produce major results have one thing in common. They have narrowed their focus. They do less, not more.

One time I was talking to a very successful salesman. This man outsells everyone in his company nationwide. I asked him, "What are you doing different from everyone else?"

He said, "I don't know, man. I'm just selling."

He humbly downplayed his gift, but I knew there was more to his story. People who are good at what they do often don't want to brag, so you have to probe deeper. I kept asking questions. "What are you doing? Take me through your daily routine."

> **If you want to achieve more, you have to do less.**

He described his routine, and it didn't sound all that extraordinary. However, at the end he added one key detail. He said, "So then I turn in all my paperwork to Mary."

"Wait a minute," I said. "Who is Mary? Is she your secretary?"

He said, "Oh no, the company didn't hire her. I did. I pay her out of my paycheck. I figured that if I spend time filing paperwork on the sales I make, that's time away from other clients. Mary is a stay-at-home mom, and I pay her a good hourly wage to handle my paperwork. That way, I'm available to my clients all day."

Wow, I thought. *This man does what matters most to his job, and that's why he outsells everyone else in the company.* Brian Tracy affirms that if salespeople want to double their sales, they need to double their time in front of prospective clients. The point is so simple that most people miss it. You may not work in sales, but if you apply the same principle to your God-given dreams, God can do some great things through you too.

People who accomplish more are not better, luckier, or more skilled; they just do less than you. You read that correctly. They don't do more; they do less.

Identify Your Core Competencies

People who delegate are able to focus on the tasks God has called them to, equipped them for, and made them passionate about. Sometimes these are called "core competencies." It takes faith to find your dream and work within your core strengths, but if you do this, I believe God will bless you.

So what are your core competencies, and how do you discover them?

Begin by focusing on what you do well. Many people spend their lives doing things they don't enjoy and are not good at. You can make a living this way, but doing so makes for a miserable existence. Does your job reflect your skills? If not, what would you have to do to get in a new position that utilizes them? Understanding your core competencies can put you on the path to finding fulfillment in what you do.

One of the reasons I rarely feel overwhelmed is because I enjoy what I do with my time. Whenever I do feel overwhelmed, it's almost always because I have allowed my attention to be diverted to areas outside my core passions and abilities.

Although I encourage people to focus on the things they're good at, there is a hazard you need to be aware of. When you focus on your strengths, you can actually get into the habit of "coasting," getting by without reaching your potential. For example, God wired me to be a teacher. This is good, because I am able to teach without preparing. (Comes in handy if I'm asked to speak on short notice.) However, this can also be a negative. I have to resist the temptation to operate on cruise control and neglect my study time. If I teach without preparing, my message may be acceptable, but it won't be nearly as good as it could have been if I had spent time diligently studying, digging deeper into God's

Word, and looking for good illustrations. If I do these things, I will teach at a much higher level.

What are you doing to develop your natural gifting? Often, the reason we stall out is not because we are outside our giftedness. It's because we never challenge ourselves to become better at what we are naturally proficient at. People who are being good stewards of their talents will read books, go to conferences, find great mentors, and increase their knowledge and expertise.

When is the last time you took a class or asked someone to critique you? One of my favorite things to do is coach people. I coach pastors on how to grow their churches, as well as coach businesspeople on how to expand their businesses and real estate holdings. When people are humble and willing to listen to others, they get better results.

The results of knowing and developing your core competencies can be nothing short of amazing. And when you find your gifts, focus on them, and develop them to their highest potential, you will discover the emotional satisfaction of knowing you are doing what you were born to do. More important, God will be able to do great things in and through you.

Look what happened when the disciples delegated the important task of taking care of the widows and concentrated their efforts on teaching (their primary calling): "So the word of God spread. The number of disciples in Jerusalem increased rapidly, and a large number of priests became obedient to the faith" (Acts 6:7).

Build Others Up by Delegating

A side benefit of delegating is that by delegating tasks to people, we help them develop. If you want to build up those around you, give them specific and challenging tasks. If you look in the book of Acts, one of the men chosen to help serve food to the widows was named Stephen (6:5). Although he had a humble beginning as a food server, he went on to be a powerful evangelist and ultimately the first Christian to die for his faith.

Think about your children. Do you want to raise great kids? Give them challenging jobs. If all your children ever do are average tasks, they will become average. If you want them to become above average, then give them above-average tasks. For example, don't give ten-year-olds tasks typical for someone that age. Give them tasks suitable for sixteen-year-olds. If you consistently challenge them, by the time they turn sixteen, they'll be able to handle the tasks of a twenty-five-year-old. When they're twenty-five, people are going to look at them and say, "Wow! You're only twenty-five, and you already own your own business?"

Then your kids will be able to answer with pride, "Yeah. I was way ahead of the curve because my parents challenged me."

Many well-meaning parents give their ten-year-olds no jobs and no responsibilities. Then when they are sixteen, they throw a fit over little chores such as cleaning their rooms. Years later, the parents wonder why their kids are still living with them as twenty-five-year-olds. We must reverse this trend and start giving our kids bigger tasks so they are equipped to become bigger people.

Consider again the story in Acts. Would Stephen and the others ever have been called to leadership if the disciples hadn't delegated the task of serving the widows? We often feel overwhelmed by all the jobs that need to be done. We forget that God wants us to delegate some of those jobs to others because he's trying to get *them* done. I'm not talking about the jobs; I'm talking about the people. People use people to get tasks done, but God uses tasks to get people done. Delegation is about getting more done, but it's also about building others up.

How do you decide which tasks to give away and which ones to keep? You learn to practice systematic abandonment.

Practice Systematic Abandonment

I love making to-do lists, but at least once a year I make a not-to-do list. I think about the tasks, jobs, and responsibilities I deal with every week, and then I ask myself which of those things I can delegate to someone else. I ask myself questions such as:

- What are the things I do at work that matter the most? (I ask myself the same question about the things I do at home and with my family.)
- What things am I doing that are keeping me from focusing on my core competencies?
- What am I doing that someone else could do as well or better?
- When I am operating at peak performance—either at work or at home—on what activities am I focusing? How can I get back to these things?

Once I've identified the jobs or tasks I need to let go of, I practice systematic abandonment. I don't merely abandon or drop those responsibilities. Instead, I seek out competent people whose gifts and strengths equip them to take on those jobs.

Right about now you may be thinking, "It sounds like you're suggesting I hire someone. I can't afford to do that!"

That's a valid objection. What do you do if you don't have the money to hire someone to help you? You may not need to pay anything. You'd be surprised at the creative solutions available if you think outside the box. For example, we often "hire" interns at our church and pay them not with money but with experience. In return for their time, we give them the experience of working at a top-notch ministry. (Okay, I'm a little biased.) And here's the crazy part. They actually thank us.

But sometimes it pays to spend money on delegating. While discussing this chapter with my wife over dinner, she told me about some friends of ours who have a twelve-year-old daughter who works as a mother's helper for $5.00 an hour. She helps mothers out a few days a week during what my wife calls "the witching hours," between 5:00 p.m. and 7:00 p.m.

One day my wife and I were having lunch with our friend Rick, who asked about our busy schedules. He recommended we get some home help, and then he challenged us to see our money as a tool to save time and enhance our relationship. Rick went on to say that when most people get a raise, they buy a bigger house or a new car. Instead, he suggested using the extra money to get some help around the home or to take the family on a vacation. By the way, we did both.

Build a Team

I'll discuss building a team in more detail in the next chapter, but here I want to point out that learning to delegate is a key step in team building. Why is having a team such a big deal? Why should you give others big tasks to do? I'll tell you why. Because as my friend Sam Chand says, "You tell me who's holding your ladder, and I'll tell you how high you can climb."

When I climb a ladder, my number one concern is who is holding the ladder on the ground level. If someone I trust is down there, steadying my ladder, I'll have the confidence to climb much higher. Who is holding your ladder? It makes all the difference. If your support team is strong enough, they will help you climb higher than you could ever go on your own.

People often ask me about the success of our ministry, and I have to confess that the credit goes to the Lord and to the team he has blessed me with. I am smart enough to know that I'm not that smart, so I hire people better than I am. I surround myself with people who know things I don't know and who have skills I don't have. I'm not afraid to ask for help. If you open yourself up to the possibility of letting others help you, you may be surprised to see the help God has already provided.

Remember what happened when the disciples delegated the task of food distribution in Acts 6: "So God's message continued to spread. The number of believers greatly increased in Jerusalem, and many of the Jewish priests were converted, too" (v. 7 NLT). Just like the early church leaders, you will become more effective as you multiply your efforts by delegating.

Before you begin this step, ask God for wisdom: "God, is there someone you have placed near me who can help me? Please open my mind to that person and give me the humility I need to ask for help."

Now, get your notebook and find a quiet place where you won't be disturbed. Then list everything you do in any given week. If you are struggling to determine how you spend your time, keep a log for a week. Once you have a list, separate the tasks into the following categories:

- tasks only I can do
- tasks I can delegate
- tasks or activities I can drop altogether

After you have finished creating and sorting your list, ask yourself the following questions:

1. What are the core tasks at work that matter the most? In other words, what am I really paid to do?

2. What are the important tasks I have at home? What do I do that matters most to my family?

3. What activities or tasks are interfering with my ability to focus on what matters most?

4. When I am operating at peak performance, either at work or at home, what am I doing? How can I get back to these things?

Next, look at your list of tasks that you can either drop or delegate. Work through them one by one and develop a plan for either delegating or dropping them. It is important that you decide both *how* and *when* you are going to follow through. For example, if you decide you need to delegate mowing the lawn to someone else, write, "This week I will hire the neighbor boy Johnny to mow the lawn for twenty dollars." As with your goals, make your delegations specific and measurable and give them a deadline.

12

Recruit Your
DREAM TEAM

· · · · ·

When my wife and I set out to plant a church that would reach thousands of people, we knew there was no way we could do it ourselves. We knew we would need a team to pull it off. And as Bay Area Fellowship grew, so did the need for a top-notch team— a dream team. You may be able to reach some of your smaller dreams on your own. However, the larger your dream becomes, the greater the likelihood you will need help. You will need a great team of people who encourage, support, and assist you.

All great successes are always a team effort. The concept of the self-made man (or woman) is a myth. Nobody gets to the top alone. Even athletes who excel in individual sports have coaches, trainers, nutritionists, and advisers, not to mention supportive families and friends. Where would a pro golfer be without a caddy? Or how about a NASCAR driver without a pit crew or sponsors?

This leads to the question, How do you assemble a great team? The answer? It all starts with you.

Examine Yourself

John Maxwell teaches a principle of leadership that is irrefutable and painful at times to admit. You do not attract who you want; you attract who you are.[1] If you are attracting less than stellar people in your life, you need to take a hard look at yourself. The best and fastest way to change those around you is to change yourself.

I often travel and consult with other churches. I've noticed that when I find a sharp pastor who is taking care of himself physically, the rest of the staff tends to do the same thing. When I meet a pastor who is sloppy, overweight, and not presenting the best version of himself, the sloppiness seems to flow over onto his staff. Simply put, birds of a feather really do tend to flock together.

> **The best and fastest way to change those around you is to change yourself.**

If you were to take over an organization you did not start, within three to five years that organization would take on your habits and viewpoints. If it doesn't, it will expel you as if you are a virus. Every great organization is the shadow of its leader. The same is true of a team.

Ask any corporate turnaround specialist the fastest way to turn a company around, and he will tell you to fire the leader and bring in someone else. That's a workable solution in the corporate world; however, if you're building a team to help you reach your dream, you can't very well fire yourself. The good news is that you can change your team by simply changing your habits.

People have a funny way of giving you what you expect. If you expect your kids to behave well, then over time they will.

If you act and talk as if you expect them to mess up, they'll probably fulfill that prophecy. What we expect from others will determine what we receive. When it comes to team building, you cannot expect excellence from people unless you demand it from yourself.

We all have areas in which we need to improve. Excellence (not perfection) is achievable. Let's take a moment to evaluate potential areas of growth in our lives. By giving attention to these areas, you can begin to attract and keep excellent people.

> **When it comes to team building, you cannot expect excellence from people unless you demand it from yourself.**

Are you staying in shape? When you take care of yourself, you send a clear message to those around you that you are choosing excellence in your life and they should do the same. You may be trying to build an excellent team, but if you're out of shape, you could be sending a contrary message. Fixing this may be as simple as losing a few pounds through proper diet and exercise. If you show the people around you that you take care of yourself, it will make a positive impression. Remember, your outward appearance displays to others a strong inner sense of stewardship.

How's your walk with the Lord? Those closest to you want to know you are the real deal. I'm not saying you have to be perfect. None of us is. But nothing will turn people off faster than getting close to you only to discover that your faith is not real. Daily moments in prayer and God's Word will keep your faith vibrant. Great leaders connect with God before they connect with others.

How are your relationships with family and friends? Great leaders connect with those they care about on an emotional level.

They are aware of what is going on in the minds, hearts, and lives of those who are important to them. It doesn't take much time to ask how your spouse, friend, child, or colleague is doing. And it shows that you genuinely care. If you want to attract caring people, you must be a caring person yourself.

Do you have a moral compass, and is it working? People who build great teams do so because those they lead respect them. Such leaders have a strong moral compass. When you behave in a way that is morally questionable, those closest to you will see it and quit following (or believing in) you.

> **Great leaders connect with God before they connect with others.**

If someone appears to be disrespecting you, take an inventory of your moral choices before you confront them. You may not like what you find. You may even discover that you are draining respect because of the choices you are making. If you have discovered that your spouse, family, or team is frustrated with you, apologize before you try to fix the situation. The most powerful words I ever say to my wife, kids, or team are not "I love you" but rather "I am sorry. Please forgive me." Most people are more gracious than we give them credit for. If you apologize and ask for forgiveness, most of the time people will forgive you and give you another chance.

When it comes to trust, everyone around you is like an ATM machine. Every interaction you have with them is either building trust (making a deposit) or taking away trust (making a withdrawal). It is possible to bankrupt a relationship by violating someone's trust. They may forgive you, but they'll be reluctant to trust you. The way to rebuild trust is by making deposits one day at a time by what you say and do.

It's Time to Build Your Team

Now that you have examined yourself, let's consider how to assemble a great team to help you reach your God-given dream. You may not be in a position to hire people, but that's not always necessary. Depending on what your goals are, you may only need to recruit family members and friends.

But keep in mind that team building isn't an end in itself. You're assembling a group of people who will help you reach your goals. In other words, this isn't like a pickup game of football in which you recruit anybody who's willing. You need to seek out people who have qualities or skills that will help you move forward.

First, your team members should share your vision. A clearly defined vision for your dream will attract the right people. However, before you assemble your team, it is only fair that you sit down with potential members and spell out where you are going. Whatever your dream is, whether it's to launch a new business, a ministry, an outreach, or even a church, if your team doesn't share your vision, you'll just spin your wheels.

Whom should you recruit? If you are single, begin by seeking out family members and close friends. If you are married, begin with your spouse. Obviously, your spouse needs to be closely involved with the direction you intend to move your life. Before you move forward, you must have a shared vision. If your spouse is not on board, God may be telling you that you need to wait and pray. Once your spouse shares your vision, then you can begin to recruit other family members, friends, and associates who share your dream.

Second, seek out people of character. An amazing story in Exodus 18 contains a practical lesson about team building. After Moses led the nation of Israel out of Egypt, he was wearing himself out. He had about two million people to manage, and he was trying to do most of the work on his own. Every day he would take his seat as a judge, and people would bring their problems and disputes to him to settle. You can probably imagine how that went. With two million people in the community, if even one-tenth of 1 percent had a dispute or a problem each day, that would be two thousand problems Moses had to resolve—every day! Exodus 18:13 tells us that Moses was sitting as a judge every day from morning to evening. Do you think he was tired?

Fortunately, Moses's father-in-law, Jethro, stopped by for a visit and observed this daily fiasco. He called his famous son-in-law aside and spoke some words of wisdom. "'This is not good!' Moses's father-in-law exclaimed. 'You're going to wear yourself out—and the people, too. This job is too heavy a burden for you to handle all by yourself'" (Exod. 18:17–18 NLT).

Jethro advised Moses to recruit men to serve as leaders under him and to hear the smaller and less important cases. But Jethro didn't tell Moses to choose people at random. He told him to "select from all the people some capable, honest men who fear God and hate bribes. Appoint them as leaders over groups of one thousand, one hundred, fifty, and ten" (Exod. 18:21 NLT). In other words, he told Moses to select people of character.

Bill Hybels, pastor of Willow Creek Community Church, says that the top three things he looks for in people are character, competency, and chemistry.[2] If people do not have rock-solid character, they will not follow through on commitments they have made. You cannot (and should not) build a long-term vision with people who lack character, or they may short-circuit the whole thing.

The best predictor of future character is past character. If you're considering people for your team and you don't know them well, ask around before entrusting them with your dream. If you are considering hiring them, get references—and check them.

Third, the people you choose for your team should be competent. Jethro told Moses to seek out "capable" men to help him. This is critical to success. As you begin to attract and recruit people to assist you, look for people who bring gifts or talents that will help move your dream forward. This does not mean that all the people who start with you will make it to the end goal. Sometimes the organization outgrows their abilities, and they must be moved into another position (always my first choice) or replaced (always my last choice).

Fourth, seek out people who are adaptable and have a teachable spirit. Suppose you start toward your goals with one strategy, but then circumstances force you to change your approach. When this happens, you need to have people around you who are willing to learn and change. They must realize they don't know everything and be willing to be reshaped without being offended.

This is when I sit down with someone and let him know the areas that need to change, and we agree on a plan of action for his performance. Yelling and screaming or simply complaining about someone will not bring the change you are looking for.

The Bible talks about confronting someone directly, and that applies to all relationships. Jesus said, "If your brother or sister sins, go and point out their fault, just between the two of you. If they listen to you, you have won them over" (Matt. 18:15). People are less resistant to change when confronted in a loving yet truthful manner.

Times change. Technology changes. Vision and goals change. Seasons of life change. A teachable spirit gives someone the ability to adjust, learn, and grow with those changes.

Fifth, your team needs to have good chemistry. Shared vision, character, and giftedness are useless if your team members can't get along. Maybe there's a person you would like to recruit for your team because she's übertalented and has rock-solid character. But then you discover that she tends to polarize the people she works with. Some co-workers like her; others can barely tolerate her. She may be perfect for your team, but if she causes friction, asking her to be on your team may do more harm than good.

Perhaps your team is very businesslike in nature, but one person is laid back. He is slowing things down because other team members must work around him rather than with him. It doesn't mean he's a bad person. It does mean he may not be a good fit. If you continue to try to force the team to work together, you not only hinder your own progress but also may be keeping that person from the productive future God has for him on some other team.

Sometimes maintaining good chemistry means you and your team need to realign. If you own a car, you know that no matter how well you drive, eventually your car will need a realignment. You feel the tires pulling in one direction or the other, and you know it's time to take it in for service. In the same way, a team can get out of alignment with your vision. Perhaps one or more team members pull away from the original plan or attempt to go in a different direction. When that happens, it's time to sit down as a group to review your dream and reaffirm everyone's commitment to it.

Unfortunately, sometimes team members are determined to go their own way. The answer to this problem is painful but unavoidable. As the leader of the team, you need to (1) confront the people who are out of alignment with the vision and ask them to come back into agreement with it, or (2) replace them. If you do not do one or the other, eventually you will find your team going in a direction you never intended. The drift may not be obvious at first, but if you ignore it, you will end up in a place far from your intended destination. Any pilot knows that if an aircraft goes off course by even the tiniest amount, on a long flight it can miss its destination by hundreds of miles.

You owe it to yourself, your dream, and the people in disagreement with you to speak the truth in love. Your vision is not up for negotiation. As the leader, you may have to challenge team members to choose between your vision or leaving the team. Doing so is difficult, but if your purpose involves an organization or a large group of people, it is necessary if you want to keep moving forward.

Cultivate Healthy, Long-Lasting Teams

The larger a team becomes, the more challenging it can be to manage the interpersonal relationships. However, difficult does not mean impossible. I have had a strong team around me for years. Like any organization, we have had turnover, but I have discovered that it's possible to minimize turnover by following three principles.

Honor Others

The way to create teams that last is by honoring people and expecting honor in return. This means you value team members and they value you.

Have you ever noticed how the apostle Paul showed respect for those who worked with him? In almost all his letters, he refers to his fellow workers in the Lord and, for the most part, speaks of them in glowing terms. He refers to a helper named Tychicus as "a dear brother, a faithful minister and fellow servant in the Lord" (Col. 4:7). In his letter to the Philippians, Paul describes Epaphroditus as "a true brother, co-worker, and fellow soldier" (2:25 NLT). In another place, Paul speaks of Luke (writer of the Gospel) and says, "Luke, the beloved doctor, sends his greetings" (Col. 4:14 NLT). Paul valued the people he worked with, and he made a point of honoring them publicly.

Valuing the people on your team is as simple as caring for them, showing gratitude for their help, giving them positive praise when they do a good job, and dealing with their shortcomings in a way that does not take away their dignity. If you make honor a part of your leadership style and encourage this attitude among your team members, you will build a long-lasting team.

Practice Faithfulness

People often talk about the seasons of life. At one point, you are a child under the care of your parents. Next, you're launching out on your own for the first time. Then comes marriage for many people, followed by a family and children. As the children grow and go on their way, you experience the empty nest season of life. And then as your own parents age, you enter a season of caregiving. Finally, as you age, you move into the final season of life, when others care for you.

Just as there are seasons in life, there are seasons in ministry. I call them seasons of blessing and seasons of faithfulness. As you may expect, a season of blessing is a time when things are going the way you want them to go. You have the resources you need. You are moving toward your goals, and nothing is slowing you down. Everyone loves seasons of blessing. However, eventually we all enter a season of faithfulness. Those are the times when circumstances are not going your way, you're facing obstacles and roadblocks, and you lack resources. Sometimes you may even wonder if you were right to pursue your dream. A season of faithfulness is a time to trust God, pray, and remain faithful to your calling.

Team members who have been with me the longest know that when we are in a season of blessing, they get the staff or the money they want for their projects. On the other hand, in a season of faithfulness, they may hear me say no to their requests. Rather than being upset, they simply recognize that it's not the right season and they must be faithful.

> **A season of faithfulness is a time to trust God, pray, and remain faithful to your calling.**

This is a good principle to keep in mind both personally and in team building. There are going to be times when you and your team will have the resources you need to move forward with your dream. Enjoy those blessings and be good stewards of your time and resources. At other times, funds and resources may be tight. In those times, don't become discouraged and be faithful with what you have. If you demonstrate faithfulness and cultivate it with your team members, you will build a long-lasting team.

Inspire Loyalty

Loyalty is rare today. Marriages are ending in record numbers. People stay in jobs less than three years on average. It seems that everyone is constantly on the move. Often this mobility is simply a fact of life in the twenty-first century, and there's not much you can do about it. However, some turnover on your team can be prevented if you cultivate a spirit of loyalty among your team members.

First, help them understand what loyalty means in the context of a ministry or team. Loyalty means you stick it out through good and difficult circumstances. This does not mean that God does not sometimes lead us to move on from a job, a community, or even a church. However, if you are looking for the perfect situation, you will find yourself continually hopping from one zip code to the next, from one job to the next, from one church to the next, and even from one relationship to the next.

The best measure of loyalty is what you do when someone hurts you or when things go wrong. It's easy to stay married when times are good, but what about when times are bad? Likewise, it's easy to stay on a team when everything is going your way, but what do you do when the wheels are coming off?

When people leave a job or a church, often their reason for leaving is that something changed. They don't like the new pastor. A new supervisor took over at work, and they don't get along. Someone else on their team got a raise, and they didn't.

Here's the problem. Everything changes over time. Change is a fact of life and a key part of growth. Sometimes the changes are painful, and that's when we face the temptation to move on to greener pastures. But if we resist the temptation and stay where we are, God can do great things. Many top executives were once junior interns who stayed with their company for the long haul. All the great pastors I know have been at their churches for decades. Great marriages are built over a lifetime.

Loyalty matters. And if you inspire loyalty to your God-given dream and encourage it among your team members, you will build a long-lasting team.

As you've been reading this chapter, I hope God has brought some people to your mind who could be part of your dream team. Get your notebook and find a quiet place where you can spend some time in prayer. Jesus set the ultimate example by praying all night before he chose his team of twelve apostles. I'm not saying you need to pray all night, but I do encourage you to spend some significant time in prayer as you consider the following:

1. What roles need to be filled on your team? (In other words, where do you need help?)

2. Who among your family and friends can potentially fill these roles?

3. What jobs will need to be contracted (hired) out?

Approach the people you would like to have on your dream team and ask them to join you. As always, set a deadline for completing this step—or at least part of it. You may not need to recruit a lot of people right away. Let your team grow as your needs grow.

13

Get the
RIGHT ADVICE

· · · · ·

In the pursuit of your God-given dream, you will eventually run into roadblocks. You will come upon situations that you feel unprepared or unequipped to deal with. Or you'll reach one of your subgoals only to ask, "What do I do next?"

When you face such a situation, the question to ask is not what but who. Who has already accomplished what you want to do? Those are the people you want to look for, because they have probably faced the same problem (or at least a similar one) and solved it. Getting good advice from the right people is critical to your success.

How do you find the right people to give you advice? There are many ways to gather the information you need. I briefly discussed some of these in chapter 8. In this chapter, we're going to look in detail at available tools and resources and how to use them well.

Books, Audio, and the Internet

It may sound old-fashioned, but the best place to start is with books. I find it amazing that people will risk their entire savings on a mutual fund or a stock but won't buy a twenty-dollar book on how to invest because they think it's too expensive. Don't think of books as an expense; think of them as an investment in your future. We should buy books, read them, mark them with a highlighter, reread the good ones, and encourage our children to read them too.

If you don't like to read but there's a book out there that will help you, get the audio book. Most books nowadays are released not only in print and electronic versions but also as audio books. Listening to a book is a great way to transform dull or boring activities into productive learning opportunities. Do you have a long commute every day? Listen to a book that relates to your dream. Do you spend a few hours each week mowing your lawn? Get an MP3 player, plug in a set of earbuds, and learn while you push your mower around the yard.

The internet has quickly become a valuable resource for learning. If you're facing a specific problem, you can almost be certain that someone else has had to deal with it. Go to Google or one of the other search engines and type in your question or problem. You will be amazed at how much practical information you can find.

For example, let's say you want to become your own boss by starting a restaurant. You've had training in restaurant management, but you need a business plan to convince a bank to loan you the start-up money. You've never written a business plan before. In fact, you've never even seen one. Where do you start? I'd suggest starting by doing a Google search on the words "how to write a business plan." Just now, I searched that exact phrase, and Google brought up over five hundred thousand hits. The same phrase on Amazon.com produced over seventeen hundred books.

We live in the information age. Whatever you need to learn to move past your roadblock, there's an excellent chance you'll find it online. But ultimately, it doesn't matter where you find your information. The key is always to be learning. Whatever your dream, if you are constantly learning and studying, you will reduce the number of places where you get stuck. And when you do get stuck, you'll be able to figure out a way forward.

Seminars and Conferences

As useful as books, audio, and internet resources are, they do have one significant weakness. You can't ask them questions. To take your dream to the next level and get past the roadblocks, you need to rub shoulders with fellow travelers on the same journey. This is why I love attending conferences. At a conference, you can often learn just as much in between sessions (by talking to other attendees) as you can from the actual sessions and speakers.

Another advantage of seminars and conferences is that they get you out of your normal environments and routines, which opens your mind to thinking differently. Sometimes you have to step out of working *in* your life so you can work *on* your life.

Depending on your level of expertise and the challenges you are facing, you may want to look for advanced workshops. These are sometimes called roundtables and are typically for those who want to go farther in their field of study. Advanced workshops can cost as much as ten times the regular conference fees; however, in my experience, the more expensive the workshop, the better the information. Another reason you should seek out advanced workshops is that the number of attendees tends to be smaller and you will be able to develop relationships with the leaders. In fact, at an advanced workshop, you may meet someone who will become a personal mentor.

Personal Mentoring

This is my all-time favorite way to learn. Of all the possible ways to grow in your skills, having a personal mentor or coach will bring the quickest results. Let's take an example from everyday life. Most of us know we should exercise and stay in shape if we want to be healthy. Suppose your New Year's resolution is to get into top physical condition, and you have the following options at your disposal: (1) read a book on fitness; (2) work out with a video; (3) buy a gym membership; (4) hire a personal trainer. Although any one of these four options can help you get into shape, which of the four will produce the quickest and best results?

If you answered personal trainer, you're correct. Personal trainers will tailor their instruction specifically to your needs. They will be available to answer your questions. They will challenge you in your weak spots. They will both encourage you and hold you accountable. Most importantly, you will benefit directly from their knowledge and expertise.

The same holds true with a mentor. A good mentor is someone who is one of the best at what they do. But they're not only good at what they do; they also love it. They have no intention of leaving their position or changing careers. They also love to help others follow in their footsteps.

Over the years, I have found that I can approach these types of leaders and convince them to help me along the way. How? Through the power of relationships.

Years ago, I asked God to make me rich in relationships. God has answered that prayer more than I ever dreamed possible. One of the secrets to the success of our ministry is that I have developed great friendships with leading pastors around the country. Here are the ways I built those relationships. Hopefully, these suggestions can help you find great mentors as well.

First, before you meet your dream mentor, prepare yourself by reading everything they have written in the past. When you meet a potential mentor, it is insulting to ask them a question they've already answered in one of their books. Also, make sure you attend their seminars and conferences, including the advanced, more intimate ones. Actually, the more intimate seminars are your opportunity to develop a relationship with the expert and cross over from conference attendee to friend.

I make it a goal to be the smallest person in the room at these events. I want everyone else there to have ten times the experience I have. I learn faster this way because I'm trying desperately to keep up with the "big boys and girls."

My college had a huge gym with ten basketball courts side by side. All the courts were filled with pickup games. At one end were the scrubs (where I belonged), those who would get cut from a junior high or high school team. The next court had decent players, the next court good players, then really good players, and so on. The players on the last court made you wonder whether Kobe Bryant and his friends had decided to stop by and play. All the players who wanted to grow were constantly trying to move up to the next court. They knew that the secret to improvement was to play with guys better than them, people who challenged them.

I love meeting with pastors of churches that are larger, more influential, and more effective than mine. This is the secret of my success (although it's out now!). I'm not as sharp as our church appears; I just keep trying to get "on court" with pastors and church leaders better than me and learn from their experience.

Many would-be leaders in business and ministry do not see the value in getting close to the experts because they think they can get what they need from these leaders' books and seminars. In some instances, they are right. But at this level, I'm not trying to discover what the top leaders are doing; I can read their blogs to find that out. I want to get next to them so I can see how they think. If I can figure out how people think, then I can apply their way of thinking to my situation. Doing so leads to bigger thinking and ever-expanding possibilities. It also kills all my excuses. It's difficult to say "that's impossible" when someone right in front of me does the impossible every day.

Motivational speaker and author John Maxwell discovered this while pastoring a small church in a small town. He began to call the offices of pastors of the largest churches in America and ask if he could take them to lunch. He offered to pay them $100 for their time. This was back in the 1970s; in today's money, it would be roughly $350. Most of the pastors agreed to the lunch out of curiosity. In the end, they enjoyed pouring their knowledge into this young man so much that most of them told him to keep the money.

That investment paid off pretty well for John Maxwell. He eventually pastored one of the largest and fastest-growing churches in Methodist history, and he became a *New York Times* bestselling author, corporate and motivational speaker, and personal mentor to CEOs of some of the largest corporations in the world.

As you begin to circulate among the experts in your field, you will eventually get to know some of them well enough to ask them to coach or mentor you. Not all of them will say yes, but when you find one who does, you've struck gold. If no one agrees, consider John Maxwell's approach. Offer to take them out to lunch and pay them for their time.

If you're not able to find a mentor through developing a relationship, you might consider hiring a coach—someone who is an expert in your field and shares that expertise for a price. Sometimes these mentors for hire call themselves life coaches, executive coaches, or consultants. Good, knowledgeable coaches can be worth every penny you pay them. However, there are a couple of things to watch out for.

Personal coaching and mentoring is all the rage these days, so there are many options available—not all of which are worth your money. I do not recommend calling a toll-free coaching network or paying to talk with someone who has been "trained by an expert." The truth of the matter is that if the person answering the phone is making ten to fifteen dollars an hour and reading from a script, you are going to find the information lacking. It's much better if you can get the actual expert to coach you. If you're going to hire a mentor, make sure they have genuine success under their belt before you give them your hard-earned money.

In addition, consultants are often former employees of companies or organizations who act as if they meant to step out on their own. Upon closer examination, however, you may learn that they were fired and are using the name of their former company or organization to lend themselves credibility. Just because someone used to work at Google doesn't mean they can help you. If they are so good at what they do, why aren't they still there?

If you plan to hire a personal coach, make sure you get good references, especially from the big names they throw around. If they are working off the fact that they helped build Apple or Facebook, you may want to call someone from these organizations for confirmation.

Although hiring a personal coach can be an expensive proposition, it can produce significant results.

Mastermind Groups

One other way to take your expertise to the next level is by creating what Napoleon Hill, in his landmark book *Think and Grow Rich*, calls a "mastermind group."[1] Hill's book (which incidentally has little to do with money and much more to do with how to be effective) chronicles the success of America's first generation of industrialists and inventors. It is no surprise that leaders such as Henry Ford, Harvey Firestone, and Andrew Carnegie were all contemporaries and friends. They would regularly share their most difficult problems with one another, and they would then generate ideas from their collective wealth of knowledge. In this way, they solved major problems and overcame almost insurmountable difficulties.

You may want to call some friends together and create your own mastermind group. A handful of pastors make up my mastermind group. I call them when I need advice, and often the ideas generated over a lunch or during a phone conversation help me lead our church to the next level of ministry opportunity.

Even if you don't start a mastermind group, you should always aim to develop significant relationships that will help you grow. If you study the New Testament, you will discover three critical relationships.

Paul was a mentor to a young man named Timothy. He considered himself a spiritual father to this young minister, helping him grow, giving him guidance, and seeing to it that others respected him. Ideally, that's the kind of person you want to find to be your mentor—someone who will care about your success even more than you do. You need to have a "Paul."

Paul also had a very close friend and associate in the ministry named Barnabas. Barnabas was an equal, a peer of Paul's. In fact, it was because of Barnabas that Paul had credibility with the other disciples when he needed it. Before he became a Christian, Paul mercilessly persecuted believers in Jesus. At first, few people believed Paul had truly converted. Barnabas came alongside Paul and helped establish him as a true follower of Christ. Barnabas knew and encouraged Paul long before he was a big shot in the church. We all need friends who come alongside to sharpen us, who can take the journey with us, and who are always there for us regardless of our circumstances. My best friend, Jay, has been my accountability partner for over twenty years. He knew me before I accomplished anything, and he loves me for who I am, not for my title or any of my so-called success. You need someone who loves you but is not impressed by you, someone who can cut to the chase with you and stand by you when no one else will. You need a "Barnabas."

Finally, you need a "Timothy." You raise this person up, and you believe in and encourage this person, just as Paul did with Timothy. This is a son or daughter in the Lord whom you pour your life into. Paul mentioned many associates, but he had only one Timothy. I am grateful to have an amazing ministry team around me, most of whom have been with me for a long time. My ministry wouldn't even exist had it not been for these people, and I am forever grateful. But it's also been my great privilege to contribute to their lives and help them grow. I'm very thankful for the "Timothys" God has given me because in order to mentor them effectively, I must constantly be growing and developing as a person and leader.

Some people will come and go in your life, but a Paul, a Barnabas, and a Timothy are there to mark you—and you them—for life.

How to Know You Are Getting the Right Advice

Now that you know how to find good advice, let's look at five ways to know that you are getting your advice from the right people.

Do Their Personal Results Match Your Goals?

Sometimes the packaging of certain books and products so impresses us that we fail to fully examine the fruit. I have heard guest preachers speak about their ministries and found myself sucked in to everything they were saying as if it were the gospel truth. But when I visited their cities and dropped by their churches (unannounced), I discovered that what they said about their ministries was very different from the reality I saw. Maybe the leaders described what they believed was happening rather than what was actually happening. Or maybe their presentations were slick infomercials that did not accurately reflect the real thing. Make sure you examine the fruit of someone's ministry, organization, business, or family before you buy in to what they are teaching.

> Make sure you examine the fruit of someone's ministry, organization, business, or family before you buy in to what they are teaching.

Are They a Practitioner or Merely a Theorist?

Before you take someone's advice on starting a business, you may want to see if they ever started one and, if so, what results it produced. If you are going to take someone's advice, take it first from a practitioner, the one who has actually done something and seen good results. In today's world of e-publishing, podcasting, and YouTube video, it's easy for people to present themselves as experts. Make sure the people you consult and look to for direction have successfully done what you're trying to do.

Are They Healthy and Do They Lead Healthy Organizations?

I've met pastors and leaders who have success but whose personal lives and organizations are not particularly healthy. I've also had the chance to meet some leaders and discover that they had undersold themselves. They were physically, emotionally, and spiritually healthy and had attracted and developed families and teams who reflected those qualities. You will ultimately become a lot like the people you listen to, so make sure they are healthy.

Are Their Practices Transferable to Your Situation?

Every situation is different, so look for transferable principles. Your goal should not be to become just like your mentors but to learn principles you can apply. Ideas are good; principles are transferable. For example, I noticed that Donald Trump buys distressed high-rises and changes their image as he refurbishes them. I can't afford any high-rises, but the principle of improvement works just as well on a single-family rental unit in South Texas as on a downtown Manhattan skyscraper.

Can You Adapt Their Principles to Your Pace?

Everyone has a pace with which they are comfortable. As you get to know experts in your field, you may be tempted to think, "I could never have or do all that they have or do." If you feel this way, keep in mind that you may be in chapter 2 of your life but you are examining chapter 20 of your mentor's life. Greatness takes time.

> **Part of success is learning to adapt what someone else is doing and creating a sustainable pace that works for who you are and where you are today.**

You can do more than you think when you look at the long-term picture. Part of success is learning to adapt what someone else is doing and creating a sustainable pace that works for who you are and where you are today.

Invest in Yourself

In his book *The Miracle of Self-Discipline*, corporate guru and coach Brian Tracy tells the story of a man who began to invest in himself. This young man was a salesman for a retail office supply house, earning roughly $20,000 a year. He went to hear Brian Tracy speak, and Brian taught that day about goal setting and investing in yourself.

Tracy challenged his listeners to invest 1 percent of their income in their own professional development. The young man took the challenge seriously and committed to investing 1 percent of $20,000 (or $200) in himself. He bought a few books and attended a local sales seminar that year and began to apply everything he learned.

The young man tracked his sales progress and began to notice an immediate upward trend. By the next year, he had earned $30,000! With an increase of 50 percent in one year, he was sold on the concept of investing in himself. That year he decided to invest 2 percent—$600—of his income. He bought several expensive sales training audio series and attended a national sales conference. The next year his income jumped from $30,000 to over $50,000.

He was so blown away by his results that he decided to invest 5 percent of his income in his own personal development. The next year, you guessed it, his income rose to over $100,000! At this point, he decided to up the ante and invest 10 percent of his gross income in his personal development. Armed with over $10,000 to spend, he hired a personal sales coach, went to several national seminars, and continued to read the latest top sales books. Within twelve months of doing this, his sales jumped to over $1 million a year.

Brian Tracy says this man keeps in touch with him and has told him that he still invests 10 percent of his income in himself, which he says is difficult to do. He has to start early in the year to spend that kind of money on himself, but he wouldn't dare not do it. He now has a sales coach, a personal fitness trainer, an image consultant, a personal investment manager, and access to the top trainers and consultants in the world.[2]

The message of this chapter is simple: get wisdom. Wisdom will protect you, guide you, encourage you, keep you from going crazy, and bring the right people around you. Get wisdom at all costs. The book of Proverbs tells us, "Getting wisdom is the wisest thing you can do! And whatever else you do, develop good judgment" (4:7 NLT). Whether you are trying to increase your income or become a better follower of Christ, the Bible teaches it and experience supports it. Get the right advice. It works.

This chapter was about getting the right advice so you can take your God-given dream to the next level. Your action step for this chapter is to search for possible sources of advice.

Get your notebook and write down the following headings:

1. Books, audio, and video

2. Seminars

3. Advanced seminars or workshops

4. Paid coaches

5. People I already know who could be my coach or mentor

6. Experts I'd like to take to lunch

Once you've written down your headings, do research and fill out your lists. As you do this, remember to think big. With God, nothing is impossible.

14

Choose to Be
A BLESSING

· · · · ·

Now that you have identified your God-given dream and you are working toward it, I want to challenge you to consider your endgame. When you begin to see results happening in your life, your newfound influence will provide exciting opportunities. Maybe you're not dreaming about becoming a millionaire; however, if you become successful in your job or company, you will receive raises or bonuses. If you are earning more, according to Scripture, your dream should also include giving more.

God does not want you to achieve your dreams so that you can have bigger and better toys such as cars, electronics, and houses. God wants you to be able to make a greater difference in the world. When we dream of what we can *have* someday, we get excited; when we dream of what we can *give* someday, God gets excited—and involved.

Whenever pastors or Christian teachers discuss giving, they face a dilemma. On the one hand, giving is a biblical doctrine, so it must be taught. However, many charlatans who claim to be doing the "Lord's work" have bilked unsuspecting people out of enormous amounts of money. As a pastor, this infuriates me.

Because I didn't want to sound like a prosperity preacher, for many years I didn't even talk about money, much less ask people to give. Then one day, while studying the Bible, I realized that I was living in fear of what others thought about me. My fears, though grounded in good intentions, were depriving people of a biblical truth. Members of my congregation didn't understand how God views money and how they should use it.

> When we dream of what we can *have* someday, we get excited; when we dream of what we can *give* someday, God gets excited—and involved.

Many Christians hear conflicting messages about money. On the one hand, they hear the enticing message perpetuated by a few extremist ministers that "if you give, you'll become a millionaire." Even a cursory examination of these preachers and their extravagant lifestyles will demonstrate who actually benefits from this kind of teaching.

Yet at the other extreme are those who shy away from suggesting that Christians have a responsibility to give to God's work. People have tried to convince me that tithing is an Old Testament concept that doesn't apply to Christians. I believe this teaching is just as wrong as the message of the prosperity preachers.

When you give, you shouldn't expect to get rich, but you should expect God to bless you financially, not only so you can take care of your family but also so you'll be able to give more to his work.

Sound crazy? Read what the apostle Paul wrote: "For God is the one who provides seed for the farmer and then bread to eat. In the same way, *he will provide and increase your resources* and then produce a great harvest of generosity in you. Yes, *you will*

be enriched in every way so that you can always be generous"
(2 Cor. 9:10–11 NLT, emphasis added).

Some people think that those of us who have big financial
dreams and desires are selfish or greedy. When someone says that
to me, I generally ask them, "How are you doing financially?"

They often say, "I'm doing all right. I get by."

I then challenge them (in a friendly way) by saying, "That's
selfish of you just to want to 'get by.'"

They look at me like I'm crazy until I explain a simple truth
to them. If we are comfortable just getting by, then we are willing to look at a hurting world that doesn't know Jesus and hope
that someone else will fund foreign missionaries. It also means
we are okay when we see homeless people or children not eating
and hope that someone else will feed or clothe them. We cannot
assume that other people will take care of these needs and keep
living as if it's acceptable to take care of only ourselves. When
you make just enough for yourself, there is nothing left to help
others. The reason behind a larger ambition is not just a larger
income but also a larger capacity to help others financially.

We can all agree that Billy Graham has had an incredible impact
all over the world. Some of you reading this have had the privilege of hearing him in person at one of his crusades, and almost
everyone has seen his crusades on television. As wonderful as I
think Graham and his team have been over the years, I'm equally
impressed with the businesspeople who covered the rent for the
stadiums and paid for that TV airtime.

How Much Should You Give?

According to the Bible, you should give as God has blessed you.
In other words, you shouldn't place a maximum limit on your

giving. However, I believe there should be a minimum. If you've been around churches much, you probably have already figured this out. I'm talking about tithing.

Have you heard of the minimum wage? This is the smallest amount a business can pay an employee. I believe Scripture teaches a "minimum giving amount." That amount is 10 percent of your income. And it should be the first 10 percent, not the leftovers.

In the Old Testament, God's people were instructed to bring 10 percent of their income to him: "One-tenth of the produce of the land, whether grain from the fields or fruit from the trees, belongs to the LORD and must be set apart to him as holy" (Lev. 27:30 NLT). Some people object to using the Old Testament to teach tithing because it was part of the law. But if you study the life of Abraham, you will see that he gave a tithe *before* the Old Testament Mosaic law was given; therefore, tithing is not just in the law but also preceded the law.

Does it take faith to tithe? It certainly does, especially if you live on a small or limited income. But the point Paul makes in 2 Corinthians 9:10–11 is that if you trust God and give joyfully, God will bless you so that you can give more. In other words, if you choose to be a blessing, God will bless you in return. The Old Testament prophet Malachi says essentially the same thing to the nation of Israel: "'Bring the whole tithe into the storehouse, that there may be food in my house. Test me in this,' says

> **If you choose to be a blessing, God will bless you in return.**

the LORD Almighty, 'and see if I will not throw open the floodgates of heaven and pour out so much blessing that there will not be room enough to store it'" (Mal. 3:10). If you trust God in your giving, he has promised to bless you abundantly, not so you can get rich but so you can give more.

Based on this truth, you should bring your tithe to God in confidence. Even if you feel you do not have enough income to tithe, you can count on God to make up the difference. When people tell me they can't afford to tithe, I tell them (based on my own experience) that I can't afford not to tithe.

If you are struggling with this, I recommend you go back to chapter 1 and rediscover that God actually wants to bless you. God wants you to have a wonderful, prosperous life that includes the ability to take care of yourself, your family, and others.

Rather than feeling guilty or apologizing for having big dreams, you should fully embrace them. The way to do that is to make sure your dreams include the systematic and regular practice of tithing. As you give, God will lead you to be able to earn more income. In fact, I have found that as you earn more, you will cross a threshold that will enable you to affect more lives exponentially.

Exponential Blessing

Many people want to earn enough to take care of their families, live comfortably, and give to their local church or mission. Those are good things, but if you are one of the few who dream of earning significantly more than the normal levels of income, then what I'm about to say is going to release you.

I believe that those who bring the tithe (the first 10 percent) and those who give a graduated tithe (increasing the percentage as income increases) will begin to have what I call exponential ideas. God will give you a business idea or an investment idea that you just can't shake from your mind. When this happens, think back over your prayer times to see if you have been asking God to bless you with resources. I have found that God blesses people with resources of the mind. He is giving you a seed idea, and he expects you to plant the seed, water it, develop it, and benefit from it. Ultimately, when that seed turns into increased income, you will be able to give more than you ever imagined.

As God blesses you and you learn to hold everything loosely and choose to be a blessing to others, God will open up more opportunities and ideas that will generate even greater returns. When the apostle Paul wrote to the Corinthian church to encourage them to give an offering for the poor Christians in Jerusalem, he said, "Now he who supplies seed to the sower and bread for food will also supply and increase your store of seed and will enlarge the harvest of your righteousness. You will be enriched in every way so that you can be generous on every occasion, and through us your generosity will result in thanksgiving to God" (2 Cor. 9:10–11).

> As God blesses you and you learn to hold everything loosely and choose to be a blessing to others, God will open up more opportunities and ideas that will generate even greater returns.

I have heard preachers make their audiences feel guilty for not giving more. It is true that if someone is not tithing, he or she is being disobedient to God. However, the new trend seems to be to make people feel guilty even after they tithe and give offerings, as if somehow everyone should live on half their income or feel bad if they want something nice. Jesus challenged people to give, yet he also is the one who said, "I came that they may have life and have it abundantly" (John 10:10 ESV).

Don't buy in to the myth that it is somehow sinful to have a nice house or car or nice schools for your kids. It is true that we should hold things loosely and give freely, but if you are one of the few who has larger than normal ambitions and is giving generously, you should not feel guilty. Enjoy your life. I suggest you follow this simple pattern. Think big. Achieve big. Give big. Then (guilt-free) live big.

A Giving Prospectus

Mutual fund companies send out a prospectus to potential clients in hope that they will like what they see and invest. Yet somewhere on any mutual fund company's prospectus is a disclaimer that says, "Past performance does not guarantee future results." These companies do not want new investors to see the mutual fund's history as a promise of what the fund will do in the future but rather as a basic indicator of what the fund's future performance might be.

God is the great investor, and he's looking for people to invest in. We know that he wants his people to give to his work around the world. Based on your past giving performance, does God have good reason to invest in you? Look back for a moment at your giving over the last year. How much of your income did you give to him?

If you have been tithing, then you have seen God's blessing. He is investing more in you because you have been faithful with what you have. If you haven't been giving faithfully, why should God bless you with more? As an investor, would you put more of your resources into a mutual fund that didn't show a return? When you pray, "God, please help me get a raise," is God saying back to you, "Why? So you can disobey me with more?"

Think about it this way. If I were to have told my wife while we were dating, "Baby, I love you, and I know we are going to get married, but I need you to sign this prenuptial agreement first," that probably would have been the end of our relationship. My wife does not love me for my money (when we were dating, I didn't have any), but she knows that love without a willingness to share *all* resources is really no love at all. God is the same way. He knows that if you love him, you will give to him and his work. Loving God is all about your heart beating for the things that make his heart beat.

When you share God's heartbeat, you cease to seek his blessing for your own benefit. Instead, you choose to let him work through you so that you can be a blessing to others.

For the Ambitious

This section is not for everybody; it is for the ambitious. By ambitious, I mean people who can't help dreaming bigger and bigger dreams. They're the kind of people who ask themselves, "What is wrong with me? Why am I always thinking about crazy levels of wealth and insanely big business ideas? Most people dream of having a career and taking care of their families, but I'm always thinking about owning properties and businesses and making huge real estate acquisitions. Why do I think like that?" It's because God needs people who think like that for his work to happen.

Let me share with you two stories about how God used ambitious people to advance his work in the world.

About five years ago, Rick, a man from my church, attended one of my business conferences. Rick was a barber. He had bigger dreams and ambitions, but he didn't know what to do with them. At that conference, Rick lit up on the inside. What I was saying resonated in his heart, and he began to ask God, "What do you want me to do?"

The first thing God told him was that he needed to tithe. Rick began to give 10 percent of his income to God, but he looked at it a little differently than most of us do. Rick felt that when he began to tithe, he was essentially going into business with God. He told God, "I'm going to tithe to you, and I'm going to ask you to bless me with opportunities, ideas, ways, and concepts so I can give even more."

He began to cultivate a dream of being able to give far beyond what he ever dreamed was possible. God began to give him ideas, and Rick wondered, "What would happen if I actually owned my own barbershop?"

Rick decided to step out in faith and start his own barbershop. Because he did not want his employer to hear the news from someone else, Rick approached him and told him of his plans. Rick then got the surprise of his life when his boss offered to sell the shop to him. They struck a deal, and Rick bought the business. His former employer remained with the business and now worked for him.

Rick immediately made improvements, and the shop started making more money. At the same time, he decided to take on a paper route and save 100 percent of the income for two years straight. He took the money from the paper route and bought into a second business. Not long after that, he bought another barbershop across town. Then he started a third barbershop and invested in another business. In five years, he went from being an employee to owning five businesses, and he was earning eight times what he had been earning as a barber.

Every step of the way he kept asking God for ideas and opportunities. He also kept tithing, even when he got to the point at which his tithe was larger than what he used to earn. He believed God was the one who was blessing him, and so with every new blessing, he increased his tithe and returned even more to God. Rather than denying his ambition, he saw it as a call from God.

If you're having larger-than-life dreams, realize that God put them there for a purpose.

Let me tell you about another guy (who also goes to my church) named Byron. Byron worked for an oil refinery and was doing very well in his job, but he wanted to own his own business. He noticed how some people were making money through government contracts, and he began to think, "What if I were to start a road service contracting business?" Byron went out on a limb, bought some used equipment, and bid on his first job. It wasn't long before he got his first contract, but it didn't stop there. Soon he had three, then four, then five contracts. During this time, he made more money than he'd ever dreamed possible, and he tithed from his increased income. God blessed him, and then he returned that blessing to God.

> **If you're having larger-than-life dreams, realize that God put them there for a purpose.**

These two stories illustrate the same thing. God gives us dreams, but he doesn't give them to frustrate us. Instead, he uses them to make his work happen. God's kingdom within us is expressed through those dreams. If you have big financial dreams, don't be ashamed of them. There's nothing wrong with living first class, provided you are also giving first class.

There are those who will want to make you feel guilty for enjoying life. And somehow we've gotten the idea that to be poor is to be godly. But the Bible does not say that. If you are an ambitious person, don't apologize for it. The only people who should apologize for their ambition and the success they have are those who are using it all for themselves.

If you read the story of King David in the Old Testament, you'll discover that he had a team of men who were his top fighters and strongest supporters. They were called his mighty men. (You can read about them in 2 Samuel 23.) Those thirty men are what propelled his kingdom forward.

In the same way, God has his mighty men and women who will propel his kingdom forward. They are the people who go to their pastor and say, "Pastor, I want to be one of your mighty men so that you can count on me when you have a special project. When you need to send more kids to camp than you have money for, call me. When you need to get that building project done, call me. When you need to expand the property lines and buy some real estate, call me. When you need something big, I want to be one of those people."

I want to challenge you to do that. And don't wait until you have the money; go before you have the money and tell your pastor, "By faith, I'm believing God is going to give the increase, and I'm going to be a person you can count on." Then as God blesses you, follow through.

This isn't about getting rich quick; it's about being responsible with the ambition God has put within you. He may want you to add a zero to your tithe, but the only way to do that is to add some zeros to your income.

Go for it. Don't slow down. Don't stop. Remember that when you tie your dreams to the kingdom of God, you tie your dreams to a rocket that will propel you forward.

For this exercise, I'd like you to spend some time brainstorming how you can be a blessing to your local church. In your notebook, write down several areas of need or special projects in your church that God has laid on your heart. Spend some time in prayer, asking God how you can be a blessing. Then ask God to provide the resources you need to help meet that need. When he increases your income, follow through.

As God increases your blessings, consider becoming one of your pastor's mighty men or women. Tell him that you want to be one of his go-to people when there is a need in the church. Then trust God to bless you so that you can be a blessing.

Epilogue

The Comeback

As you move toward your God-given dream, it's all but certain you will experience setbacks. When that happens, don't be discouraged. Setbacks are simply God's opportunity to give you a comeback. When failure comes your way, you may feel helpless, but you aren't. You can pick yourself up from defeat and win again. One of the best examples of this is King David.

In chapter 8, I referred to a biblical story in which David faced a great failure. He and his men had been off at war. When they returned, they realized they had made a critical mistake by leaving their families unprotected and vulnerable to the enemy. They returned to find their homes burned and their wives, children, and possessions taken. They had lost everything. David's men were furious and even talked about stoning him. But 1 Samuel 30:6 tells us that "David found strength in the LORD his God."

David could have just quit right there. After all, his dream of becoming king wasn't going well at all. He had been branded a rebel, and he was constantly on the run from Saul, who still held the throne in Israel. Now a band of raiders had attacked and taken everything he and his men cared about. Even worse, his men were turning on him.

Up to this point in the story, everything was doom and gloom. But there was something the enemy could not take from David, and he cannot take it from you either. He cannot take your attitude. He cannot rob you of your faith and belief in God. You see, between everything that happens to you and what you do about it lies a small space that makes the difference. It's a place called choice. When you experience failure and defeat, you can choose to dwell on your pain or you can choose to plan your comeback. It's up to you.

Rather than let circumstances overwhelm him, David found strength in his God. He chose to focus on the things that would encourage him rather than the obvious negativity around him. Instead of wallowing in his pain, David did something about it. He sought the Lord. David prayed, "'Should I chase after this band of raiders? Will I catch them?' And the LORD told him, 'Yes, go after them. You will surely recover everything that was taken from you!'" (1 Sam. 30:8 NLT).

David waited on the Lord for a specific answer to his question. He could have gone after the enemy in a blind rage, but more was at stake than just the recovery of family and possessions. David's future role as king—and quite possibly his life—depended on him making the correct decision.

Just a few days before I wrote this, a man in my church told me about a prayer time he had when God began to move powerfully within him. He asked me to help him understand what had happened. I told him that when you approach God, it is exciting, but when God approaches you, the experience is unforgettable. When you know you have heard directly from the Lord and have a specific word from him, you have a newfound confidence that will lead you to change your entire situation.

If you are facing insurmountable odds or a major defeat, you need a breakthrough. This does not mean you should try to break through to God. Rather, you should wait on the Lord until he breaks through to you. And once he does, you need to act.

After hearing from God, David and his men took decisive action and went after what they had lost—the people they loved so dearly. The problem was that they had no idea where the raiding party had taken their families. Nevertheless, they pursued the enemy, and as they went, God provided further direction.

David and his men came upon an Egyptian man who was a slave of one of the enemy soldiers. The man had fallen ill and had been left behind to die. After David gave him food and water and guaranteed his safety, the former slave told him where he could find his family. David and his men were able to locate the enemy and their captured families because they now had an insider helping them.

Many times we do not move forward because we are waiting on God to work out everything in advance. This is a critical mistake. If David and his men had delayed in their pursuit, the Egyptian man may have died in the desert. They would have lost the one person who could help them rescue their families.

God will give you his Word before he gives you his break. In other words, he will tell you what to do, but you should not expect provision until you move in obedience. You must act in faith and move on his Word alone. When you take decisive action, this act of faith will release God to give you his break.

I call these breaks the miracle middle. It's as if we are standing on one side of a cliff and need to get to the other side, and God tells us to get a running start and jump. Like most people, we immediately say, "God, are you crazy? If I jump, I will fall."

But God says to us, "When you jump, I will immediately place my miracle middle, the bridge you need, to get you to the other side."

The miracle middle, or the break you need from God, will come only after you begin to obey God's clear direction. Your faith is what activates God's miraculous hand on your behalf.

After a long battle, David and his men recovered everything: their families, their possessions, and their honor. In addition, David received a bonus. His men—who had recently been talking about stoning him—saw him develop into a great leader.

David experienced many setbacks, yet he never stayed down. Failure and tragedies come to everyone. Like David, the winners in life handle them differently. They don't stay down; they rise up again.

Every great leader goes through tough seasons. That's why we sometimes call them seasoned leaders. Great losses and personal defeats are not meant to stop you but to give you an opportunity to trust God and establish your leadership legacy. When you follow God, he will give you his Word and expect you to act on it. When you do, he will bring his breaks and give you the victory. He allows the setback—for your comeback.

Now that you've worked through this book, you are ready to pursue your God-given dream. And the only way for that to happen is for you to move forward in faith, trusting God to guide, provide, and (when necessary) restore. It's time to stop thinking and act. Your dream lies ahead of you. Today is the day to pursue it.

Notes

Chapter 1: Is My Dream from God?

1. Brian Dozeman, *Sales Insights from a Herman Miller Watercarrier* (Lincoln, NE: iUniverse, 2006), 52.

2. Rick Warren, The Purpose-Driven Church conference lectures (audio).

Chapter 2: Think Big, Then Think Bigger

1. Dan Lier, *The Ten-Minute Coach* (audio).

Chapter 3: Transform Your Dreams into Goals

1. Mark H. McCormack, *What They Don't Teach You at Harvard Business School* (New York: Bantam, 1984).

2. Rick Warren, The Purpose-Driven Church conference lectures (audio).

3. Napoleon Hill, *Think and Grow Rich* (Meridian, CT: The Ralston Society, 1937).

Chapter 4: Change Your Beliefs

1. William James, in Brian Tracy, *Change Your Thinking, Change Your Life* (Hoboken, NJ: John Wiley and Sons, 2003).

2. Richard Bach, in Gary McGuire, *Realizing Your Potential* (New Delhi, India: Epitome Books, 2009).

3. Brian Tracy, *Change Your Thinking, Change Your Life* (Hoboken, NJ: John Wiley and Sons, 2003).

4. John Maxwell, *Success* (Nashville: Thomas Nelson, 2008).

Chapter 7: Develop the Action Habit

1. This quote is attributed to Woody Allen, from an original interview in the *New York Times*, August 21, 1977.

2. Robert Allen, *Multiple Streams of Income: How to Generate a Lifetime of Unlimited Wealth* (Hoboken, NJ: John Wiley and Sons, 2000).

3. T. D. Jakes, spoken in several of his live sermons, recorded at the Potter's House.

4. Walt Disney, as quoted at the end of the movie *Meet the Robinsons*, 2007.

Chapter 8: Strengthen Your Confidence

1. Zig Ziglar, *See You at the Top* (Gretna, LA: Pelican, 1975).

2. Shad Helmstetter, *What to Say When You Talk to Yourself* (New York: Pocket Books, 1982), 20.

3. Ibid., 21.

4. Bil Cornelius, *I Dare You to Change* (New York: Guideposts, 2010).

Chapter 9: Build Momentum through Diligence

1. Malcolm Gladwell, *Outliers: The Story of Success* (New York: Little, Brown and Company, 2008), 35.

2. Brian Tracy, *Eat That Frog!* (San Francisco: Berrett-Koehler Publishers, 2007), 3.

3. Henry Ford, quoted in *International Encyclopedia of Prose and Poetical Quotations*, compiled by William S. Walsh, 1951.

4. The concept of "stop, start, continue" was inspired by an Outreach Conference lecture by Pastor Miles McPherson of the Rock Church, San Diego, CA.

5. Jacob Bernoulli, quoted in Gary S. Goodman in the audio series *The Law of Large Numbers*, a Nightingale-Conant presentation.

6. Grant Cardone, *The 10X Rule* (Hoboken, NJ: John Wiley and Sons, 2011), 1.

7. Ibid., 2.

Chapter 12: Recruit Your Dream Team

1. John Maxwell, *The 21 Irrefutable Laws of Leadership* (Nashville: Thomas Nelson, 1998).

2. Bill Hybels, *Courageous Leadership* (Grand Rapids: Zondervan, 2002), 61.

Chapter 13: Get the Right Advice

1. Napoleon Hill, *Think and Grow Rich* (Meridian, CT: The Ralston Society, 1937).

2. Brian Tracy, *The Miracle of Self-Discipline*, a Nightingale-Conant presentation, 2010.

Bil Cornelius is the founder and lead pastor of Bay Area Fellowship in Corpus Christi, Texas, which has in just twelve years grown to a membership of over nine thousand people between ten campuses, making it one of *Outreach Magazine*'s Top 100 Fastest-Growing Churches. In 2008, he launched Bil Cornelius Ministries, a TV ministry that brings his message of hope to South Texas. He can be seen hosting the *Praise the Lord* broadcast throughout the world on TBN. Bil is also a sought-after speaker and church health and growth consultant and lives in Texas with his wife, Jessica, and their three children.